FRESH

How to Chan
By Men and Wome

DENNIS BARKER

ROSTERS LTD

‘I find that quite a lot of the men being referred to me by doctors, often in their forties or early fifties, come with the question: “Is this man deteriorating?”

‘And my feeling, which is awfully difficult to prove, is: “No, this man is not deteriorating. He has just been in the wrong job all his life.”’

– *Junior hospital doctor working in psychiatry, who changed her own job in middle life.*

Published by ROSTERS LTD
60 Welbeck St, London, W1.

ISBN 0 9480 32 69 3

Designed and published by ROSTERS
Typeset by JH Graphics Ltd, Reading
Printed and bound in Great Britain by Cox and Wyman Ltd, Reading

First edition 1990

Contents

INTRODUCTION

The oppressive symptoms may vary deceptively.

Perhaps a feeling of tiredness in the morning even greater than the one at night. Having to brace oneself before walking into the office. A jaundiced view of colleagues. An absence of joy in one's family and friends. A lack of concentration in big things and a lack of grace in small ones. An inability either to work well or to relax easily afterwards. A growing sense of certainty that one's life and job are of no significance.

However varied the symptoms, they may all point to one human condition which is unfortunately too common and about which society still cares too little. Not illness, not even general boredom, but simply and specifically being in the wrong job and not knowing how to change.

This is a book about people who *have* changed their careers when it would normally be regarded as too late, mostly in middle age. Many people today *have* to find alternative jobs as the result of redundancy or early retirement. This can be a liberating as well as a depressing experience – and one which will happen to more and more people in an era where the concept of 'a job for life' is disintegrating and more people may have to retrain for different jobs. But most of those I interviewed had taken their vital step voluntarily.

How do you tell whether the yearning for a different sort of job is valid or not? So much has been written about mid-life crises in both men and women that it appears to be very unfashionable *not* to have one. A general feeling of unease and discontent around middle age is indeed common and must be lived through. But it concerns me here only to the extent that it may *mask* a very real dissatisfaction with the choice of a career that, perhaps, should have been acted on long before.

This is the vital question that a person who feels wrongly slotted must ask himself: is the feeling to be taken at face value, or am I simply experiencing a disenchantment with my job and everything else as the result of advancing age: a disenchantment that must be weathered until the storm is over? Supplementary questions can help give a pointer. Did I feel definite rumblings of discontent with my job long before middle age, but suppress the feeling because I had other things on my mind, such as raising a family? Was I a little uneasy about the nature of my job even when I was regarded as a great success at it, or did the feeling come on when – perhaps because of a change of executives above me – other favourites took the limelight?

It was the people who had answered all these questions in a way which suggested that their unease was real, both objectively as well as subjectively, whom I sought out. I wanted to know their state of mind when they realised things were wrong, plus when and how they had determined to do something about it.

I also wanted to discover how they felt while they were turning their working lives round and how they coped; and whether they thought, at the end of the process, that it had all been worthwhile.

In the dozens of interviews I conducted I did not discover anyone who, as the result of a late change of career, had gone on to high fame or fortune, and it would be misleading to suggest that change can or should always produce more money.

Often money is simply not the point. A woman journalist had a well-paid job, requiring specialist knowledge, on a quality national newspaper. She liked the actual writing work but not the circumstances in which it had to be carried out: 'I didn't like the total package – working in anyone else's organisation. I was egocentric enough to think that if I did my work well enough, I didn't see why anyone else should interfere with it.'

This sort of freedom from interference is not on offer in the newspaper world, where work can be, and is, cut or altered by others without consultation to suit space or other considerations. She went into business as a publisher on her own account, resisting even more lucrative offers to stay in newspapers. It was some time before she made as much as an entrepreneur as she had done as an employee.

'But then,' she said, five years after the conversion, 'I wouldn't say money was my motivating factor.'

Many people who go into jobs because they are lucrative discover, an ulcer or two later, that in fact money isn't really *their* motivating factor, either. I found that many people I interviewed had changed to 'doing-good' jobs in the broadest sense, not always because these jobs, being on the whole more modestly paid, were those that were more easily available, but because they wished to wash the taste of the money-hunting rat race out of their mouths. Some, while staying within this rat race, had taken definite steps to bring more altruistic activities into their lives: for some, palliatives can amount to a fresh start.

But, having talked to many who obviously did genuinely need a complete change, I am convinced they are great in number, and that they are heavily burdened by a frustration they can barely understand, let alone remove – certainly not without the realisation that there are many other people in a similar plight. They need moral support in their feelings and intentions – possibly even more than precise information about how to change course.

At 25, a man or woman 'knows' his life is bound to change for the better. Things will fall into place. He (an expression which, for the sake of brevity, also includes 'she') will come into his own and be taken at his own estimation. At around 45, he knows his life has not changed, or not changed enough; and that it won't change unless he makes it change *now*. It is now or never.

That is how he feels. It is a very real and vivid experience.

Can he change it? It is a feeling which tends to go round in circles inside his own head. Can he remove the sense of being wrongly slotted? Can a surveyor become a social worker or vice versa? Does he really know what change he wants? Has he the energy? Dare he risk the loss of security – and of face? Can he command the confidence of those he wants to employ him in a new capacity, and carry his own family with him? If he has to accept a lower standard of living to do something he really wants to do, will his children lose respect for him? Such questions abound and drain the energy that could otherwise be used for change: little wonder that many embryonic changes drown entirely in this bleak ocean of questioning and self-doubt.

It is a pity that society itself (especially at times of industrial and commercial re-organisation, redundancies and unemployment) does not take a more active hand in fitting round pegs into rounder holes. It is worthless to use this fact as an excuse for doing nothing on one's own initiative; but it *is* a fact.

People who are wrongly aligned, who feel they want to do something other than what they are doing, are a social waste. Not as extreme a waste as if they were totally unemployed, but a waste nevertheless. Society itself, and its needs, is becoming increasingly fluid and shifting. Factories close here, and open there. New techniques are introduced, old ones abandoned.

Hundreds of jobs exist today which were unknown fifty years ago; some traditional occupations are actually short of practitioners. But the individual is still largely expected to make his personal progress in one way only:

by climbing just one professional ladder. The only alternative to this is coming down that ladder, and this may well come about with the slackening of purely youthful energy, the competition of younger people and the facing of administrative changes which may victimise a man in middle age in spite of his own merits.

In the main, we know of only one alternative to an infinity in the same working groove: the scrap heap. It is a gross and unforgiveable squandering of human potential. All honour to those men and women (like those that appear in these pages) who have beaten this rule by their individual efforts. Their story should encourage the rest.

We are living longer. Medical science devotes time and effort to this end, while the result of living longer is often that the person who experiences it does so as no more than a cruelly extended period of depression and waste. It is quite senseless, but society has not yet tackled the problem head-on, and shows too few signs of doing so.

There can be a mental condition in which progress and creative change appear to be impossible. This may well occur at the very time when the children are growing up and becoming independent, and when progress or change in the parent is therefore especially desirable. But the engineer is not expected to become the parson. The stockbroker is not expected to become the civil servant. They may wear a tired mask, but not a new one.

The more nervous energy such a misplaced person has, the more he may work against himself. This may sound like a paradox, but it is true.

His energy will feed only his self-doubt. He may be told vaguely by friends to 'think positively'. But there is something frightening in a positive thought when it could well lead to a precipitate exit from a thankless job which nevertheless does provide the daily bread. Depression may be adopted as a 'safe' refuge when initiative seemingly offers only a worrying and uncertain prospect. It is not really surprising that, with society's connivance, people tend to shy away in middle age from their potential for change and growth, at the individual cost of unhappiness and the social cost of wasted working potential and wasted doctors' and psychiatrists' time.

Educational systems must take their share of the blame. Almost all careers, and the ways of life that surround them, derive from circumstances obtaining, and decisions taken, at the age of fifteen or earlier. In spite of educational changes this still largely applies. A man may go into the wrong job because of this. Square pegs in round holes cannot always be detected at once. The square peg may not even realise it himself; he has not had the chance to acquire a yardstick of satisfaction or happiness. Youthful energy can tackle almost any job, even an unsuitable one, and get something out of it. Other factors at this stage tend to disguise the true situation. Social contacts outside the office, or in it, take the edge off any unease caused by the work itself. Then family responsibilities – providing for children and so on – make re-thinking difficult and acting on it impossible. Creative satisfaction in one's children enables one to postpone estimating the creative satisfactions of one's own life.

In middle life, all these palliatives may be withdrawn almost simultaneously. Social engagements no longer hold the excitement they had in youth. Children have grown up and moved away, leaving a gap. Perhaps that gap has made the marriage itself look less attractive and relevant. So the middle-aged person looks at himself and may fall victim to a sense of redundancy and martyrdom unless he can now modify his own life positively in some way.

During my interviews with people who have been able to do this, I heard more than once the admission: 'I now had to think of myself and for myself, and I had forgotten how to do it.' It came from women even more than men.

Truth can sometimes be cold, if necessary, comfort. It may well be that it is out of vacuums such as I have hinted at here (and found in the subjects of my interviews) that creative growth comes. Perhaps it is out of the agonies of self-doubt, not out of the smugness of confidence, that crucial changes in lifestyles are made. This is the irony and the hope. But it is not easy to believe in it while the gloomy phase is in possession, *unless* one can draw on the practical example of other people. This is a much more useful commodity than arid impersonal advice, which must always have a limited value in highly individual decisions.

By and large, the people in this book have applied themselves successfully to the task of turning negative feelings into positive gains and changes. Their successes and their mistakes are equally revealing and, I hope, helpful. I did not have to bring pressure on them to make them talk. They expanded with interest and relief into the story of their changes. They wanted to talk. Few interviews lasted less than an hour, even if the person concerned had said beforehand that he could spare only a few minutes. Most people I saw were able to suggest further people for me to see; there is a tangible unofficial freemasonry amoung people who have changed careers.

To encourage frankness, I have thought it best to quote individuals only by Christian names – fictitious ones. A few of the people I talked to may have felt they did not want what they thought of as their vulnerabilities linked with their present selves.

Perhaps this was because of their fear that younger people might hold their difficulties in contempt, but I hope this book will be of relevance to younger people as well. I hope it will encourage them to be more understanding and welcoming of changes in other people's later lives. They may thus make job changes in middle life more socially acceptable and more easy for themselves when *their* turn for doubt and reassessment comes.

The man of 25 'knows' *he* will never be 45. He will. He will.

CHAPTER ONE: WARNING SIGNS

A fifty year-old occupational therapist was talking about herself when she was still a secretary-receptionist.

> 'I wasn't getting any further. All my family were doing things. My daughter got a degree. My sons were obviously going to university. I felt I would be typing until I was 65 and that would be it.'

It was a familiar sort of story, but she did not know that.

Miriam – a thin, highly strung woman prone to self-reproach – twisted her hands together at the memory. Her school had been a girls' college, where she hadn't worked, because she was 'just lazy – conscientiousness came to me later in life, when I thought it was too late.' She hadn't got any A levels, or even any O levels.

> 'Yes,' she said, 'it was an important influence on me, the fact that my children were now grown up and going out and doing things . . . I was very discontented. I felt I would always be the tea-maker and the rusher-abouter and I was getting older and working in a medical group practice as secretary to a social worker who was younger than I was.'

I nodded as she spoke: a nod of recognition. I had heard the same sort of story many, many times, with only the names, sex and details changed. I told her this, and it encouraged her to go on.

'Then we engaged another social worker in the department. She was even younger than the first one had been, and I was getting older. I was 49 and I was secretary to a social worker who was in her late twenties. It started to make me feel older than I was. It was such a nice atmosphere in the department, everybody had a team-work approach to things. It was just . . . I suppose it got monotonous for me. All the typing of endless case histories and things like that. Endless telephoning. I could see no end to it.'

Suddenly she brightened. 'I think it was good, looking back, that the job was becoming more boring and the people I was working for were getting younger,' she said. In this, she was probably more clear-sighted than others who find themselves still in this debilitating, but surprisingly frequent, situation: being trapped by past failures or omissions into an increasingly unsatisfactory and edgily unsuitable job.

'Yes,' she said, 'it stirred me into doing something. Four years ago, I wrote off to the physiotherapists and the occupational therapists. I realised I could never make a physiotherapist because you have to know physics at A level, and I am not very good at that. So I took up occupational therapy. I went to the School of Occupational Therapy in Hampstead. I had to write out a curriculum vitae of what I had done in the past, as I hadn't got a School Certificate. In this case, I don't think it made much difference that I didn't have A or O levels, because I had a long history of working with a medical and social work background.'

But her mood when she first went back to school, a student at fifty, could be summed up in one word: petrified.

'Yes, I *was* on the first day,' she said. 'I felt what it

must be like to be black or in any minority group. At one point I just took my sandwiches and ate them outside Swiss Cottage Baths. I felt I simply couldn't cope on that first day.'

Miriam, the secretary-receptionist for a trade union and foreign trade delegation before she turned to occupational therapy, was expressing what most people in her sort of situation feel: growing resentment. Determination to cut adrift and try something more satisfying. Frightening insecurity at the initial impact with new circumstances, especially the jolt of being a 'pupil' again, not a wage earner with an established (if resented) identity.

The adaptation test

The Squadron Leader employed with a charity retired from the Royal Air Force a little early after a heart attack had blocked an expected promotion. He was just fifty. He was offered, via a relative, a job as a cashier in a sub-branch of a bank. He took it because he had applied for several civilian jobs, been shortlisted for some, but always failed to be selected. After being appointed to the job in the bank, he kept looking.

'I went for a constabulary administrative job in one of the county forces. I think there were 180 applicants for the job and I was on a shortlist of three. One of the three was the retiring superintendent from that county force. Guess who got the job! This sort of thing happened many times, at least half a dozen. I found that appointments were really filled before the shortlist was considered. It was a demoralising period. I was in the bank for 2 years; and I spent 1 year, 364 days looking for another job. I loathed it because it was routine. It was low-grade work, quite well-paid for what it was. I was virtually doing an office boy's job for a man's money. I was thoroughly dissatisfied with what I was doing – I had no job satisfaction whatsoever. I found adapting to civilian life difficult in this job.'

And that, surely, was proof of its unsuitability: conversion to the *suitable* is rarely that difficult.

The Squadron Leader was lucky in that, ultimately, he did not have to work out his own salvation. The Resettlement Branch of the Ministry of Defence kept sending him offers, for which he made applications. Eventually he applied for the job of number two to the director of a medical charity, and got it.

> 'It was a big change,' he said, 'but I took to it like a duck to water, because it was a chance of getting one's teeth stuck into an opportunity or reorganise something. It had responsibility.'

His will to change his circumstances was augmented by arrangements not available to those in ordinary civilian life who feel they are square pegs in round holes. The fact is that people thinking of changing their jobs – and with them, perhaps, their whole way of life – do need encouragement and help, if only moral; but they find it difficult to get it. Society is hard on those who wish to change jobs after the age of 35 or so. Well-meaning friends, too, will 'sensibly' try to talk one out of it, ignoring the fact that unhappiness at work can make life hell not only for the worker but for everyone around him. All the pressures say: stay put and bear it.

The limitations of 'gumption'

Very few of the people I approached to tell me about their

experience in changing jobs refused to talk to me. The most emphatic was a hospital doctor, a late entrant in her profession.

> 'I do not think there is any point in my seeing you. If someone has not got enough drive to change their career in middle life for themselves, they won't benefit from anything I can say. If you don't know the possibilities for yourself, if you don't have that degree of gumption, then you are not going to win.'

I think she was wrong. Most of the other people I talked to thought she was wrong. They welcomed the chance to talk about what had been a demanding watershed in their lives. They believed it would help others by way of example, and so do I. They wished that more guidance and moral support had been available when they made their own particular changes.

The subjective feeling test

Usually the desire for *more* personal significance comes at the very time when the person in an unsuitable job is experiencing *less*, because he senses that possibilities of change and development are receding, and that younger people are taking over in his existing field.

Paul, the branch accountant and deputy branch manager of a bank in the North of England, had been in banking twenty years when it occurred to him that he could be in banking for another twenty years, and that he disliked the prospect.

> 'The next step would have been a branch of my own, then probably one or two other small branches in different parts of the country, and that would have been my life. I felt I wanted to make a more

significant contribution, so I moved into the building society field. This used to be a service industry, helping people to buy homes. But now, the building societies look at one another's figures every month, and get extremely neurotic about them. They are putting more and more young men into the field to rush around madly, to buy money by the use of commission payments. They are vying with one another in a terrible way. So the building society movement, which started off with this wonderful idea of helping people to buy their own homes, is very big business. Perhaps it is rather like a church: sometimes when it grows, it doesn't keep the same values. The element of service that attracted me to it had gone . . . It is rather sad, but this changing pattern has appeared, as it appeared in banking, which was a servicing industry but is now a profit-making operation . . . I was looking for something more personally significant.'

Eventually he found it, as general secretary of a housing charity, by first taking a £3,000 a year drop from his building society salary. His lowest psychological moment was when the second-hand car he had bought for the job broke down by the roadside and he had to try to thumb a lift: he, a man who had previously had a company car, regularly serviced.

'But I think I am a fairly resilient person who can usually rise above such situations,' he said. 'I should have been very frustrated if I had stayed where I was. I saw almost a duplicity, a kind of basic dishonesty, in business today. You have to sell the customer what you've got and try to fob him off. This, I think, is something that charitable life hasn't inherited yet.'

John had a well-paid job as assistant marketing manager of a subsidiary of a nationalised industry after leaving university. He was earning a salary far in excess of what most young men of his age were getting.

> 'In theory it was a job with a purely commercial pay-off, but in practice I managed to change it slightly through circumstances. It was the first time this post had been created. Its main object was market research and advertising where we were selling our products, which hadn't really been done before. There were other things that made the job more interesting than it might have been. For instance, we moved our headquarters. The whole of the time I was there, a lot of attention had to be given either to the build-up to this move or the aftermath of it, and I was dealing with that side of the operation. I had to recruit new staff and help train them with the staff who had been found other jobs by the Board when they didn't want to move. That was a very interesting side of the job, recruiting people and training them while teaching myself the job. The sales office manager resigned at that time, so I was doing his job as well as my own *and* learning his job and teaching his successor. That was fascinating. I was that busy, I couldn't get bored with the paperwork side. Too busy to bother with the fact that this wasn't really what I wanted to do. The fascination of the moment had made me forget that.'

Once he knew that his attempts to transfer to the industrial relations side would come to nothing – the Board at that time had a policy of recruiting its personnel managers from the trade unions, which paid off in terms of industrial peace – John became so generally bored that he 'couldn't wait for the days to end'. The symptoms will be familiar to everyone who has been in that situation.

> 'I looked forward to the weekends. I wanted to get away in the evenings and do my own thing. Before,

> I generally took some work home with me at weekends and I didn't resent going to work on Monday morning – I was quite happy to go. By the time Sunday evening came, I was perfectly happy to get back to work because there were things I wanted to get on with that I felt needed doing. All that went. Monday was a *drag*. By Tuesday I had managed to adapt to the drag and I could survive. But I couldn't wait for Friday. On Friday afternoons, it was largely clock-watching. At five, I was out of the office.'

This was a subjective feeling. Many ambitious young men would have envied him his position. It did not matter. The feeling that he was misplaced began to affect the standard of his work and, more marginally, his social life.

> 'I doubt very much, at that time, whether my performance was good or even up to the standard required,' said John. 'I was delegating far more. I was delegating far more than I should have done. I was getting shot of the jobs I was bored with, giving them to someone else to do because I couldn't be bothered with them, frankly. They seemed quite pointless as far as I was concerned . . . Socially it began to affect me to some extent. If shop was talked among colleagues in the pub, I tended to wander off. It became rather uninteresting. At work I think that, on the whole, I didn't snap at people or anything like that, but I found it increasingly difficult to get on with my immediate superior.'

John took a charitable job which earns him less than half what he would be earning if he had stayed in his Organisation-Man job in the nationalised industry. But because he feels he is running his own show, and doing some good for people, and because he feels that the financial side may change sufficiently for the better to make it economically tolerable, he feels twice the man he was.

Physical hints

Sometimes the psychological warning signs are not obvious. At least, not until afterwards. The warning light may come through something physical, like a coronary attack.

It did in the case of Robert, first an accountant in industry, then a consultant in accountancy and management, and then a parson. He made the change to the Ministry when he was over fifty.

> 'I had a pretty hefty coronary in 1963, having been on my own for three years,' he said, a slow-spoken man with a cautious glance but no visible signs of internal strain. 'I was in hospital in London and just let the world recede and started meditation. I was in for five weeks, and that was my green light to change my career. I had been driving hard as an independent consultant, as you have to. And I was cut off from people. When I was an accountant in industry, I had my own office to look after. I was dealing with personal as well as accounting problems. Having become a consultant, that went. One has to remain a little aloof with clients, obviously. Coming to parish work, I regained what I had lost in becoming a consultant – dealing with people. I found being grafted on to an organisation very demanding. One is working at peak pressure all the time, with very little support at all, really. One is on one's own. I am sure that this was part of my coronary.'

In a large number of people I talked to, the *sensation* of being alone was one of the symptoms of being wrongly, or at least inadequately, slotted in one's career. People seldom feel alone in jobs to which they are ideally suited, even if they are physically on their own in them.

The escapist fallacy

A distinction must be made between gravitating towards an occupation one prefers and merely trying to escape from the demands of the job one is in. Most of the people I talked to who had successfully changed their jobs said that in fact they had got *some*, or even considerable, satisfaction out of the job they were in. They had applied themselves to it as best they could and made the experience as positive as possible. It is a personality characteristic (a determination without self-pity) that bodes well for the venture of changing one's career.

Most organisations who accept late entrants have a vigilant eye for escapists, and weed them out. This is particularly true of charitable organisations and religious orders of any description, which attract numbers of people whose recommendation for a new job is that they collapsed under the strains of the old one. Robert insisted that his own evolution from accountancy and management consultancy to the Ministry was not a form of escapism.

> 'If it had been, I would not be in this seat talking to you today,' he said at his rectory near a new town. 'I don't regret the first part of my life in the least; I wouldn't have missed it. I did not regard myself in the slightest as missing personal satisfactions. It was just that nothing is more powerful than an idea whose time has come. That is putting it in a nutshell.

Talking to monks, they will say, "I never *wanted* to be a monk. I just felt I *had* to become one." Well, I just felt I had to become a Minister. It certainly wouldn't be true of me to say that I collapsed and had to withdraw from active competitive life. I would not accept it, either, of many monks I know. In fact, in one convent I know very well, they make a strong point of putting all novices through psychiatric screening before they take them. Because if they show any sign of escapism or general failure to cope, they will not be accepted. Courses for those going into the Church are very severe on people who appear to be only opting out of what they are already doing. The feeling of being successful in the job you are doing is a recommendation to becoming a priest. Perhaps in some other spheres a feeling of failure can be part of the process of going towards another way of life, but I don't think so from the priesthood point of view.'

But if a political party agent or a brush salesman, who thought he had hidden vocational leanings towards the Church, also felt that his present life was a hollow failure, wouldn't in fact that be a good sign? Robert thought not.

'If you found yourself in that position you would have to go back in your mind to see where you had made a mistake. What were you rejecting? If one is a Christian, then one obeys the will of God. If you do obey the will of God, then you are going to be satisfied, even if you are selling brushes at the door. If you are dissatisfied, you have to work out why. Is it because you have rejected God? Only by going back to the point of rejection, and attaining acceptance, would you then be able to go ahead again. Anyone who is selling brushes and feeling a failure is probably dissatisfied because he had rejected God in his life. The answer for him is not necessarily to become a parson.'

The test of the validity of the desire to make this particular change, said Robert, was to check it with other people. They would take a more objective view. 'Anyone who opts for the change on his own volition is suspect. You have got to get others to agree.' This objectivity test has a more general application. Any desire for a change of career may not necessarily be discussed with other people – one of the signs of determination may be a lack of interest in doing so – but it must emerge, ultimately, in a precise, concrete form that *could* be discussed with other people. This is a test which will weed out mere day-dreaming.

Creative dissatisfaction

If over-indulged, dissatisfaction can become a substitute for action. It can also antagonise acquaintances and put off people who otherwise might help. But, if kept in reasonable check, dissatisfaction *can* be a useful signal to send out in a situation in which a simple switch of temporal jobs is envisaged.

Gerald's was such a case. After giving up the theatre because it had no financial security and he had just got married, he found himself running a businessman's club where his in-laws lived.

> 'I spent ten months doing this, but it was obviously not my scene. I was very happy on the members' side of the bar but not on my own. I didn't like being behind the bar. You see a side of life *across* the bar that you would rather be part of. I used to think to myself, "It is better to be a fool than have to suffer

fools gladly." I suppose my attitude did show sometimes. There was a member of the club who owned a factory. He could see I was very dissatisfied. He suggested I go to him as a trainee manager, which I did. I did it for about a year, went to night school, got the City and Guilds in manufacturing; and all this at the age of 33.

The rut test

The *feeling* of being in a rut is often a sign that the job in hand is the wrong one. Routine is seldom noticed *as* routine in a job which the individual concerned finds interesting; every piece of the jigsaw is looked at and valued for its own sake, and every moment is lived through for itself, without that escapist living in the future – of which clock-watching is the most obvious and telling example.

George, who became a probation officer at the age of 43, was very conscious of a rut when he was still a panel-beater.

> 'I suppose by the age of thirty I had just about built almost every type of motor car which was built by hand – Rolls-Royce, Bentley, Allard, Bristol. I had done much experimental aircraft work. And you begin to realise that, if you have been ambitious enough to try all these things, then – unless there is something pretty revolutionary coming up – you have just about tried everything in your own trade. I am now 51. Would I have been more frustrated and dissatisfied if I had stayed in engineering? I don't know. I think that eventually – going by the others that I have seen – you get in a rut and you accept it. There comes a time in one's life when you have to assess whether it is your ambition to go on, or whether you can have tranquility of mind which

would be just as rewarding as material gain. I doubt if I could have had that tranquility of mind if I had gone on in the engineering business. You see, it may be said I am in a rut now, because I have come to the conclusion that being a probation officer in the field, and not an administrator, is what I want to do for the rest of my life and I am happy to do it. I have been in it for eleven years. But I don't *feel* I am in a rut. Perhaps, before, I was having some sort of kick at the ball of life. But now I feel I am kicking at it all the time because of my clients. I feel I am in touch with reality through their problems. I believe in reality therapy. Probably the most difficult thing for most of us to face up to is the utter reality of our situation. This has to be put over to my clients in a very gentle and careful way, very often. Nevertheless I don't see it as repetitious. That reality, and their aims for the future, are what life is really all about.'

The outsider sensation

The sensation that your mind is not fully stretched, and that you are on the outside of events in which you would like to participate, is only slightly less desperate than the feeling of being in a rut. It is the starting point for many job changes.

Stephen was a successful freelance journalist working for national newspapers and magazines. He is now a solicitor. He insists that he never disliked journalism, and has no wish to imply that journalists as a professional body are mentally lazy.

'It was like this,' he said. 'If, to keep alive as a freelance, I had to do jobs I didn't really want to do, what was the point of being a freelance? But by temperament, I am not an Organisation Man. I think there was another thing about journalism which I won't say I disliked, because I never disliked the job. But what made the thing seem tedious to me was that one was always doing things at second-hand, in the sense that you were always writing about what *other people* were doing, asking them what *they* thought. This can become frustrating. I enjoy many aspects of journalism: the technical aspects of subbing and writing captions and, later on for me, cutting television film and writing commentaries. But there is nothing more boring than, say, waiting outside the Trades Union Congress to see what has been decided at some meeting when you know nothing *has* been decided, but you will have to do a story just the same. I felt I was getting older. I must have been thirty when I started thinking like this. I felt that if I wanted to have a new career I had better do something about it quickly. I wanted something that would stretch my mind a little more. I wouldn't suggest that journalism is a particularly mentally lazy occupation. But it is not difficult once you master the craft. I wanted something where I personally felt I had to put more into it . . . There is no doubt that I am more interested in what I am doing now than if I had stayed in journalism. I am interested in what I do. Not every second of the day at work. One has boring stretches, inevitably, if you do any job. But, generally speaking, I am glad I made the move. A lot of people think that a lawyer's work is boring. I think that is because they haven't done it.'

Right and wrong tiredness

Being emotionally and physically drained, *and resenting it*, is another sign that a change is overdue. Lewis is now a probation officer and previously a stockbroker's clerk, said he was 'not sure' which job drained him more, but he was quite sure there was a difference in the way he reacted to being drained.

> 'I think every day when I was in the stock market I got awful blood pressure. So, in physical sense, that drained me,' he said. 'In an emotional sense, I find being a probation officer very, very draining too. I am aware that sometimes when I am interviewing clients I am mentally turned off because I am processing, in myself, the emotional pressure they have given me after a long day at work. I might see seven or eight clients a day. The problem is that one cannot really plan, because you get clients coming in suddenly, perhaps at critical times, and they make enormous demands on you. These sort of clients, who make enormous unreasonable demands on you, are often so deeply deprived and disturbed that one can't really make any effective plans for them. They have little insight. So that part of it can be a draining process. But the point, as I see it, is that I *gain* more energy from doing it than I did from what I used to do. This may sound odd, when I have just said that I get very tired. But I wake up the next morning feeling recharged and really wanting to go back and have another go, to try another approach.'

This is often the test of the suitability of a job: is the tiredness temporary or permanent? Does sleep restore the desire to 'have another go'?

> 'Before,' said Lewis, 'I was very much a façade, presenting very little of me as I think I know myself. I was someone in a reasonably sleek suit driving a fairly smart car, putting on enough of an impression

> to win over someone's confidence in order to get some business. This job is nearer my true self. I think I am probably presenting myself to my clients more sincerely here. If I am annoyed or cross or tired, or feeling shabby or scruffy or something, I can acknowledge that and perhaps share it with them. It is not always a one-way process. It is not always listening to your client. Sometimes you can turn it round to good effect.'

In other words, the freedom to be frank is often a test of whether one is in the right occupation; a feeling that one is playing a role is a sign of incompatibility. If the job is suitable, the necessary self-presentation will not *seem* to be an imposture, but merely part of the craft of the job.

Pay and promotion warnings

Excessive concern about pay and promotion prospects may not indicate pure ambition so much as the simple unconscious realisation, and resentment, that one is in the wrong job.

Ben, who moved from draughtsmanship into teaching when he was over forty, realised that something was basically wrong with his working life when he moved from one draughtsman's job, where he got no promotion, to another job which was little better.

> 'The firm was fast expanding but, instead of promoting me to a higher position, they brought in somebody who wasn't even an apprentice-trained draughtsman, and they paid him about £6 a week more than I was getting. A similar thing had

happened at the previous firm. They always seemed to bring in people who didn't know as much as we did about the job. This seemed to be the trouble with being a draughtsman. If you are a good draughtsman, they keep you drawing. If you are not such a good one, then they make you a foreman or chargehand or a ship's manager and push you out somewhere. It wasn't necessarily the best workers who got the best situations.'

No doubt there was some objective truth in Ben's claim. It was nevertheless indicative that he was trying to climb the wrong ladder. On the strength of the experience of many job-changers I talked to, it emerged clearly that a ladder on which your particular personal qualities are not likely to get you promoted, or on which you do not really *want* to get promoted, may well be the *wrong* ladder.

The flitting syndrome

Flitting from job to job is a warning sign. Ben had jumped from job to job in draughtsmanship with increasing frequency. Had he stayed in draughtsmanship, he estimated that the moves would have become more rapid and his frustration more pronounced.

'Yes, I think I would have flitted more and more. I flitted in the first place, six months at a time, to get a reasonable job, and that was fair enough. But then I became steady for something like nine years. Then it was three years. Then I got to two years, then one year. I think by now I would have been flitting from job to job in a matter of months. As soon as I got fed up with a particular job I would have left and gone out and got another one. I think almost certainly, in the past six years when I have been teaching, that had

I stayed in draughtsmanship I would have gone through at least three or four jobs, perhaps many more. But now I don't feel as if I want to move at all. I have applied for deputy headships, but I wouldn't want to be a headmaster, because a head is an administrator only, whereas a deputy is still a teacher, and teaching is what I like doing.'

The respect drain

Decreasing respect for the aims and objects of one's own organisation or craft is one of the more visible signs of unease and wish for change. At first, the job that William (erstwhile journalist and then a barrister) found was made for him.

> 'What happened,' he said, 'was that, purely fortuitously, my wife saw an advertisement in *The Guardian* from a charity wanting a publicity director with a knowledge of the politics and economics of a certain part of the world. I fitted the bill exactly. It was made for me. It was a very interesting job, raising money for the resettlement of refugees. It involved me in writing, it involved me in speaking. It was a very tough and demanding job and it suited me. I did it for four years. Then I found I wanted a change. It was a very exhausting job, but that was not it. In a sense I enjoyed the writing, I enjoyed the creative part. But let me put it this way: I really had very little respect for what goes under the guise of public relations. Maybe it was my journalistic training, but I saw through a lot of the work I was connected with. There wasn't an overt split between my employers and myself. But I had a certain discontent about methods and techniques.'

In short, William was not by temperament a public relations man. He was in the wrong job. Had he been a born public relations man, he would have regarded the methods as simply the unavoidable means to a good end.

Drift towards inessentials

People who are caught up in the mainstream of their work rarely get caught up too much in peripheral concerns. Roderick, now a social worker, got off on the wrong foot, as a watchmaker, simply because he was a refugee in Britain in the war, and was advised by his foster parents to learn a trade. It was a sensible move from the 'practical' point of view, since Roderick's command of English was not perfect.

> 'But,' said Roderick, 'I found it more and more uninteresting. I was less interested in watches than in people. I developed what I thought was a stomach ulcer, but it wasn't. I certainly grew a lot of neurotic symptoms: fatigue and so on. I wasn't really interested in shopkeeping. I wasn't very interested in making money. As a shopkeeper you have to squeeze as much as you can out of your customers, or you don't do it very well. And squeezing people wasn't my idea. I liked the diagnostic bits of the job. I would be 26 when I started my own shop. But keeping a shop was of no interest to me. I had no interest in great window displays. I found talking to customers much more fascinating than their watches. I sometimes talked to them about their own problems. This is not the way you make a fortune.'

Nest fouling as an art

Few workers in the right jobs have a consistent resentment of their employers. Real hatred is almost certainly a sign of being wrongly slotted. Mike had worked in industry, with an 'every morning a Monday morning' feeling for several years when he breached his company's confidentiality in a way that made the sack inevitable.

> 'I think it was an unconscious way of trying to get myself the sack,' he said. 'I am the sort of person who doesn't take decisions easily or lightly. Really, I suppose I am like a lot of human beings: I am lazy. I would rather have a situation forced on me than make a firm decision. I think that, psychologically, that was what I was doing in this case.'

He was unconsciously fouling his own nest so that he had to get out of it.

The quietness test

At least Mike took some kind of *action*, albeit unconscious. The ability to take action is in itself a sign that the discontent in an unsuitable job is very real. It is easy to harangue and day-dream.

> 'The hallmark of a man who is actually going to do something about an unsuitable job,' said Mervyn, now a vicar and formerly an insurance auditor, 'is a quietness and not a sensationalism. I would say the things that indicate that a man is in fact going to take the step is a quiet resolve and persistence.

People who start off with a great deal of ballyhoo and enthusiasm which doesn't last, get nowhere. I can think of some young men who have said they would like to go into the Church. They think, when they say that, of the garb and the books and a lot of show. But this is the very thing that normally doesn't guarantee it will last. The sure sign is the *persistent longing to do something*.'

The friendship indicator

If you are employed in industry, but most of your friends are actors, writers and newspapermen, it could be a warning. One of the signs of being ill-suited to a career is that your friends are all in a quite different one. We may accommodate ourselves *consciously* to the people we work with, for the sake of their comfort and our own. But in choosing friends, it is the unconscious mind which is at work. It may give a more true indication of what we really are and what we really like doing.

Liking people in other careers is not an *infallible* indicator that you are in the wrong job; it may mean merely that you are looking for variety, a change of type of companion in your leisure hours. But it can, taken with other things, be a clue. It was – or should have been – in the case of Bryn, now a successful architect. At school and at university, he set out to be a physicist – a mistake.

He found the work increasingly unpalatable. It bored him. It was either too difficult to do, or it was tedious. He became convinced he had made a big error in studying physics, though he rather liked the biochemistry, because he found the science of life itself a fascinating subject.

'There were a few things to sustain me at university'

> said Bryn, 'including some friends from *outside* my own subject. They were all reading English, music or mathematics. It struck me as significant, even at the time.'

It *was* significant. He knew by the time he left university that he had made a mistake. But by then it was too late to escape. He felt trapped. The thing that freed him from the trap was joining the Navy, to do operational research at sea as a civil servant. He made friends with an architect he met at sea, borrowed all the books on architecture he could find, and did a lot more drawing. At school, he had been told that it was no use him wanting to be an architect, because he was not especially good at art (a *non sequitur* propogated rather less frequently today). As a scientific civil servant, he got himself transferred to the Building Research Establishment. 'Immediately,' said Bryn, 'the link between science and art, that I had always looked for, began to happen.' One of the signs that he was now better suited was that he began to make friends within his own job.

> 'I had found a marriage of the two fundamental human activities – *knowing* and *doing*. I met a bunch of scientists who were fascinated by architecture and architects who were fascinated by science. There were more people in the world like me! We became friends and they are my friends to this day.'

Bryn studied art once more and got himself into architecture. He was lucky. It is wiser to recognise the warning signs of one's friendships, or lack of them, early on and to act on them.

Paradoxically, getting on *well* with some people – especially at impressionable periods of one's – life may be misleading as a guide to our own talents and consequent choice of career. A bad teacher, for instance, may put us off a subject for which we have a natural aptitude (and so distort our careers), but a *good* teacher may give us an inflated view of our own ability in his subject (and just as surely distort our careers).

It was so in Bryn's case. Because his physics master happened to be an inspirational force, he made his pupils think they had more ability in his subject than they actually had.

> 'I thought I had much more potential as a physicist than was really the case, because he made the whole subject so fascinating,' said Bryn. 'But I soon saw that as a physicist I would not go high enough to break through the boring bits to the really imaginative heights.'

So, though human relationships may be a guide to whether we are in the right career slot or not, it is as well to bear firmly in mind that they *can* be misleading. For every man who has changed his job because he didn't like the people, there is probably another one who has stayed too long in an unsuitable job because he *did* like the people, and allowed this to blur his unease with the job.

Ultimately it is the doing of the job itself, irrespective of the human elements surrounding it, that will make or mar satisfaction.

Uncreative aloneness

Suddenly feeling that your human relationships are insufficient for your personal needs may be a sign that there is not enough creative satisfaction in the job. It is perhaps sad, but nonetheless true, that people who are bound up in their work voluntarily tend not to notice human relationships, or their absence, quite so much.

Albert, a marine engineer who gave up his job when

he was 32 to go to university, said he thought that the move, and time itself, had made him easier in personal relationships. As a marine engineer he was away from home a lot, and he began to resent it. On average he was away three months out of four, and he became aware that there was no time for relationships.

> 'That is one of the things I found so disturbing when I came ashore at first. So many contacts had been lost. I did not have roots. I wanted to be in contact. I was never at home long enough to join organisations. Since I have come ashore it has been a source of satisfaction to find these communications building up again. I have met others who came ashore and had to go back. I can quite easily say that I have never had a second thought. I have never had any inclination to return.'

There is one further fact, almost certainly significant, to be said about Albert at this point. He became a marine engineer in the first place not because it was his own choice, but because all his family had been marine engineers. Would he have been so worried about personal relationships if in his bones he had felt the job to be suitable to himself as a separate person? Should he have resisted parental influence earlier? The point is worth separate examination.

CHAPTER TWO: THE FAMILY PRESSURES TRAP

Stewart still maintains he was never close to a nervous breakdown. His wife is not so sure.

'My lowest psychological point,' he said, 'was when my wife was saying how ill she thought I was. Depressed. Anxious. She said that she was worried.' Nervously and revealingly, he shied away from any suggestion that her fears may have been real.

Superficially viewed, Stewart's life was following an easy, predestined course free of the pressures to get-on-or-get-out that afflict the self-made man. He was in the family business. The principal of the firm was his father. His younger brother joined the firm after he did. Stewart was therefore the heir-apparent to the well-established and lucrative family business, but his state of mind did not correspond, even in his own eyes, to this rosy external picture.

> 'I felt I could get myself through what I had got to face,' he said, 'simply by pushing on and getting by somehow. My wife thought I might have a nervous breakdown. Have I accepted this? I have accepted that the thought I might have a nervous breakdown was her opinion. It wasn't mine. I wasn't prepared to admit to being tense or irritable. It was a situation I found myself with, and I just had to live with it. You either get worse or you stay as you are and get rid of the problem.'

In his own eyes he was facing a situation he had just to soldier through; in his wife's estimation he was on the edge of a nervous breakdown; in the world's eyes he was a man with an easy career supported by family advantages. What was the truth?

The truth was that Stewart was the victim of what I discovered in a high proportion of people who had changed their jobs in middle life. *The family pressures trap*. It afflicts people at all social and intelligence levels. It happens through the highest of motives and the lowest, but it can be wantonly destructive in terms of real career prospects and peace of mind.

Stewart's father exerted his pressure for a very common reason; a reason that can be, however, in these more democratic days, increasingly life-consuming. He himself had joined the family business, and he wanted his eldest son to carry on the line. It is one of the most direct and dangerous family pressures, for it offers a tangible carrot and an appeal to 'safety' and common sense. It is also one of the most destructive, for if the business alignment works out badly, then family relationships are strained as well, and the unfortunate victim of the family pressures trap has no peace either at work *or* at home.

This was so in the case of Stewart, a gentle, guarded man who unconsciously revealed just how poisoning the family pressures trap can be by talking about this aspect of his career very guardedly, and insisting that neither his real name nor the organisations he has been connected with be named; all this many years after the family business relationship had in fact been severed.

On leaving grammar school, his father told Stewart he wanted him to join the family firm as, eventually, a partner.

> 'This I agreed to do,' said Stewart in his quiet voice, 'knowing very well that I was going to go into the Services at a fairly close date, because the war was on. I don't know that I *wanted* to do it. But my father

> was rather demanding about it and the interviews I had organised for other jobs didn't come to anything. He made it very clear that he expected me to go into the family firm. There was very little option for me to do anything else.'

He spent two years with the family business. Then he went into the Services. After three and a half years he returned to the family business.

> 'I started off being dissatisfied. I had had three and a half years in the wild, though under discipline, in the Forces. I liked being in the Forces. I don't know that I had any preconceived idea what I was going to do after that. Going into a very small organisation, I felt terribly confined. But then, I am not sure what else I would have been able to do.'

Of course Stewart never had a chance to find out what else he could do. The family pressures trap closed round him again. His father pleaded, plausibly, that his presence was needed.

> 'There was my father and his partner and the two girls in the office. I made the fifth member of the organisation. I think probably the turning point in that part of my life was when my father's partner died and he had to find another one. He took me into partnership – a simple partnership and I was a silent partner. I wasn't a full partner for several years. But then things began to look up a bit and so did my financial return.'

This gave more scope for his interest in the company, so that he was not tempted to sit down and ask himself the vital question that should be posed by everyone approached to join a family business: if it were not my father who is approaching me, would I see this career as suited to my own temperament and character?

> 'The more responsibility I got, the better I enjoyed it. I have to be very careful not to condemn my father. But I think that probably any family business has its problems. Until you marry you are in the same house, as a rule, as your father. If you are working with him, you are in the office with him all day. And we tended to stick fairly close together, as the business didn't keep to normal office hours. It ran on Saturdays and Sundays and at all times. It was something that you got used to doing. I think you become familiar with it. It just becomes the pattern of your life.'

As he recalled all this, Stewart's manner was not that of a man with a double-barrelled name and the confidence of coming from a family of substance. It was that of a kindly, well-disposed man who had never really established himself as a personality in his own right, and was even now fearful of talking straight to the point about something which had, latterly in the partnership, made his life a misery.

The pattern became increasingly troublesome until it came to an end *22 years* later. By then it had absorbed all Stewart's youth and not given him the time or space in which to make cool objective judgements about what, or who, was wrong.

> 'My younger brother had entered the partnership, and my father was still there. I suppose that as I got mature, I realised the increasing problems of working closely with the family. I felt that it was almost too introverted. All one's eggs were in one

basket and there was perhaps not enough scope. There were probably a few family disagreements. My idea of doing something may not have been the same as my father's or brother's. So we disagreed over it.'

I had to lure Stewart over the next revelatory hurdle. Did his father and his brother agree more with one another than he himself tended to do with either?

'Well, I think so. I think that my brother and my father tended to see eye-to-eye more than I did. And so you got a situation developing where the third person is out on a bit of a limb. I felt increasingly isolated.'

There was then, in Stewart's words, one of 'those silly incidents which do happen.' His father came round to see him at his home one night. He was angry with Stewart over 'something which I had refused to do as far as my brother was concerned – it was almost a domestic disagreement rather than a business disagreement.'

But business and domestic matters were combined. Stewart was not prepared to climb down on the issue (which he would not discuss, and which, for the purposes of this book, does not matter).

'I am not sure what the relationship was between my father and my brother. But, almost from that point, I think my brother tended to take a stronger line with the business. We had an attempt at a takeover. My brother particularly wanted it resisted, whereas I wasn't so determined – and even less so as the price offered went up. I knew of the difficulties in proving to those shareholders who were willing to accept the bid that it was justified to resist it.'

An impartial observer, viewing the situation with a new eye, might well have suggested to Stewart at that time that his greater willingness to sell out indicated a lesser business compulsion than that possessed by his brother. There was no such impartial observer. There rarely can be in a family business.

The points at issue between the two brothers then widened, as is often the case. Stewart went abroad to discuss business arrangements. His brother later overturned some of the arrangements.

'All that happened was that he seemed to alter every arrangement I had made. And he started criticising some of the work I had been doing when he got back. This criticism was the straw that broke the camel's back. It was at this stage that I started looking for another job, unbeknown to my wife. When she discovered about this, she was wholly in agreement with my course of action and also involved herself in trying to find something for me to do. I was 49. I thought I might "get through" if I stayed with the family business. But, on the other hand, the prospect of another fifteen years of having to toe the line in the way I was expected to toe the line was something that I wanted to avoid if I could.'

Why should the elder brother toe any line? Was his younger brother a forceful man? Stewart's hesitancy showed how deep the remaining scars still were.

'He is very dogmatic in what he says and what he

wants. Whether *forceful* comes into it, I am not sure. The business seems to be very successful at the moment.'

Eventually Stewart found the way out of an impossible situation. He applied for five jobs that he saw advertised, was offered two, and accepted a job as an officer of a charity.

The financial sacrifice was considerable. He and his family had been living in a house which had been valued at £50,000, but which, in a property slump, they had to sell for £43,000. It had five bedrooms, two bathrooms and a garage for three cars. He moved into a house which cost £25,000 and had three bedrooms. With the capital thus released, he augmented his income, which had dropped to just under £2,400 from around £7,000. (These figures bear no relation to current values.)

The family made do with clothes that would otherwise have been replaced. They were careful with lighting and heating. On the other hand, working for the charity, in a small office located in a private house, he did not need to buy smart clothes any more. 'I just go and buy another pair of trousers and make do with the jacket I have got,' said Stewart. 'We are very free and easy in our outfit here.'

Many men might have been demoralised by such a change in his financial circumstances. Stewart was not.

'I felt I had a burden off my shoulders,' he explained as we lunched together on rolls and cups of coffee in a serve-yourself café. 'I am fortunate in that my wife and I have outgoing personalities and were determined to make the best of it. My wife had a part-time job in the end, and had an income of £300 a year. But that was more to fill her time than to eke out the finances. We had moved to a new area where our social life was nil. We had no meetings to go to of local organisations, and we were obviously not going to get involved in as many parties and glasses of sherry as had occured in the place where we had lived for many years. And to some extent we tended to avoid invitations of that sort to begin with, until we found out whether we could afford to do it.'

His sense of relief at getting out of the partnership was overwhelming. For the first time in thirty years he felt able to lead his own life. He didn't have to think about being telephoned in the evening or at weekends. He was able to make arrangements for a pension, which the family business did not offer. (Many do not.) He had escaped being turned into 'a rather well paid office boy'.

Delicately I enquired why he thought he had allowed this humiliating process to happen. It seemed the key to the question of whether in the first place he had been suited to the role assigned to him by his father.

'I think it is a softness in my character. I wouldn't like to call it a Jekyll and Hyde situation, but in some ways I am a fighter and determined to do things either for myself or for other people. On the other hand, I am not prepared to charge about when I think it is a lot easier to be quiet and perhaps take the path of least resistance. That sums it up in a few words.'

And (a factor he has in common with many people who have made the changeover to charitable work) he said he did find it easier to fight on *other people's behalf* than on his own. He liked helping people to solve their problems. This personality characteristic, so potentially creative, can be a liability in many more competitive occupations.

The encouraging point to anyone in the same position as Stewart is that he does not regard his business career as having been a waste of time, even though sometimes it was a torment. Stewart feels powerfully that he is better suited to charity work than to business, but doubts whether he could be effective in it had he not had the business training at the start.

> 'I got a very wide commercial and general knowledge. I had had so many things to cope with that it is now easy to deal with almost any situation that comes up.'

The father who despised learning

The point has general application. Almost all the job-changers I interviewed said they had gained something from the occupation they had accepted as the result of family pressure. Many had used it as a more direct stepping stone to their future careers than Stewart managed to do.

Gary is such a case. Here, also, the pressures were to join a family business – a small coachworks. The encouraging point of his case is that, although his job seemed further away from his ambitions (an academic life) than Stewart's, the bridge found was not only more direct but involved less financial sacrifice.

Gary left grammar school with a School Certificate. He was a boy with a quick academic grasp, and his teachers assumed he would be one of the four or five in the class who would go to university. Instead he left school at sixteen.

> 'At that time, I would rather have gone on to university. But my father thought the family business was the thing, so that was what I did. We dealt with motor body building. This was just after the war. Vehicles were in very short supply. You couldn't in fact get new vehicles without a two or three year

> wait. You could keep a car for a couple of years and sell it for a greater price than you paid for it. That rather produced a market for special vehicles like shooting brakes. And at the start of the war, every large vehicle was commandeered and the back chopped off and an ambulance body or truck body put on it. The reverse process took place after the war . . . My father's argument was that the line of academic study I was pursuing was irrelevant. There was strong psychological pressure to join the family business.'

Gary has learnt from this experience and made sure that his own son was not lured into the same misalliance. His eldest, aged 25 at the time of our interview, actively asked to come into the family business when he was 18. Gary resisted it, partly because at that time he was considering leaving it himself, but also because he thought it would not be fair.

> 'To come into the family business after you have outside experience is one thing. But to grow up in it, I don't think *is* fair. I never felt my own man. I never had any outside terms of reference, which I think was a great loss.'

But the family business was booming at the time his father persuaded him to join it, which helped to undercut his own independent resolve. He found his first experience of commerce traumatic, because his father insisted, quite rightly given the decision to join, that he would do the average apprenticeship including the most menial jobs, just as if he were not the son of the boss.

> 'So I did it,' said Gary, 'though it seemed like a waste of schooling to me, even at the time. I was not using any of the knowledge I had acquired. I was starting a completely new line of country. It was very good

training: I learned every aspect of the business. I was also progressively taking charge of the administrative side of the business, the office work and so on . . . The office side grew and grew with the increase in red tape that came in with all the rules and regulations that were to be introduced.'

The red tape was to be part of the catalyst that ultimately prised Gary loose from his prison. In the meantime, one of the things that enabled him to reconcile himself to the business was the thought that in due course, when he 'settled down', he would have sufficient spare time to undertake private study and get additional qualifications.

The time did not materialise: it seldom does. Gary, always with the yen to study, confessed that he felt cheated. 'Yes, just a little bit,' he said, with the determination, typical of the person who has succumbed to family pressure, not to blame the family too much. (It is healthier and easier to blame an unsuitable employer who has no family connections with you.)

'I just wanted to learn: I enjoy learning. I enjoy studying. But it didn't happen. I didn't have time. I got married and had a family fairly young. I was twenty-one when I married, and had two children fairly soon after. This kept me pretty busy . . . The dream gradually began to recede.'

He was conscripted into the Forces for two years, and found that he quite enjoyed his first contact with the outside world. Afterwards he hesitated before going back to the family business. 'As I had cut free of it, I was very tempted to do something else,' he said.

Again, the family pressures trap snapped shut. His father offered him more money to come back. After a conscript's pay, it was attractive. He succumbed, especially as he had nothing positive lined up as an alternative.

'I am,' he explained, 'a fairly steady sort of chap. It takes me a long time to decide on a change. But once I do decide, that is irrevocable.'

Gradually outside circumstances helped focus his mind on the change his unconscious mind always wanted. He became interested in the designing part of the business, and correspondingly aware of his lack of paper qualifications of any sort other than the General School Certificate. Extended legislation meant more paperwork and more 'red tape'.

There was a subtler pressure, and one that is more revealing of the presen-day plight of those who have given in to the pressure to join small family concerns – the type in which the siren call, 'You are really needed', is the most likely to be seductively plausible. The social standing of the small businessman started to change.

> 'When we started as a family business,' said Gary, 'an employer was recognised as *someone* in the community. But our way of life gradually changed this, so that the employed man was the one who seemed to be getting the upper hand. When I say upper hand, I mean gaining the recognition and the rights. Every bit of government legislation affecting industry seemed to be for the employee at the expense of the employer. The pearls of business were progressively whittled away, so that it became less and less attractive to be your own employer. The responsibilities and the risks were much greater and the rewards were smaller.'

Whether Gary's social analysis is correct or not is irrelevant. Even if he were rationalising a general discomfiture in the job he was in, it would merely prove that he *was* uncomfortable in the job, and that people in such a position tend to dramatise the fact in many different ways, most of them more easy to admit to themselves and discuss with others than a resentment against family pressures.

Gary found himself at the age of forty, which he saw as the turning point in any man's life, with the feeling that he had reached stalemate. He was not progressing. The business was not expanding, but the time it was demanding from him was not shrinking. Larger manufacturers were providing strong competition. And, perhaps above all, there was a certain amount of friction with his father. Officially he had retired, but after three months he came back into the business, on an ostensibly part-time basis.

> 'Even at the age of thirty-odd I had the feeling that I had never achieved independence. On paper, yes. But morally, no. I was always being criticised for something or other – most of the time unjustifiably, I thought. And he used to go home and tell my mother all sorts of tales. He was a bit deaf, so he always used to get hold of the wrong end of the stick and go home with a garbled version. And my wife would come along and say, "What is this going on?" All that sort of thing. It became rather tiresome. Anyway, I was beginning to think, "I am not realising my ambitions . . ." So this brought me up to the stage where I was approaching forty and I was progressively feeling I was in a rut and didn't quite know what to do about it.'

It was building on one of his practical activities in this period of frustration that led to his eventual escape.

He became involved in the educational field on joining an organisation concerned in a comprehensive schools dispute that was affecting a school his own youngest son was likely to attend. At the same time, his daughter was at training college, studying to be a teacher.

The two threads merged. Gary became the governor of a local school. Part of his work was to interview teachers for jobs.

> 'I very much thought, "You know, I may be very new, I think *I* could do that job just as well as you could, and I think I would enjoy doing it." I felt I was decidedly on the wrong side of the fence, though I was enjoying what I was doing as a school governor very much. At that time, they were appealing for mature teachers and I thought, "Here is my chance! I think I could perhaps do something about further education." I was always thinking about it.'

But he moved tentatively at first. Few people who actually change their careers, as distinct from dreaming about doing so, appear to be the sort of people given to hasty decisions in sublime moments of blazing clarity.

He made enquiries; saw a man he knew at the local College of Further Education; realised that he could not get into university without A levels and that he could not get A levels and run a business at the same time; came to the conclusion that the only possible exit with the qualifications he had was via teacher training; and, cautiously, decided that a course that would involve him in engineering science would be the most profitable means of utilising his previous experience.

He took a course in what is now known as design technology at a college 150 miles from his home. He chose the college partly because it was in a pleasant area and partly because it was within weekending distance of his home, where he decided he would go at weekends to complete the formalities of disposing of the family business: he had had a good offer.

The certificate he took required three years at the college. He had a small grant. The family was largely off his hands – his daughter was at the teacher training college, his eldest son was just completing his course at a local technical college.

> 'Everything seemed to jell right. It was a Now or Never decision. This was when I was 42. I had to make up my mind pretty quickly. I did some quick negotiating and some quick thinking. I sent an acceptance of the place at college, on the basis that if the worst came to the worst I could always cancel it. I went ahead with the sale of the business. It got to the stage where I had got to do something to break out of the vicious circle. Some guys change their wives, some guys change their jobs. This is the sort of age when people do *something* to get out of the rut. I thought, "If I don't do something, I shall be changing my wife". Domestic circumstances were getting very strained. I thought, "This is really not the way, I'd better change my job". And things worked out very satisfactorily from then on. I never regretted it.'

After initial fears about 'going back to school', Gary found he settled down well, helped by the fact that at that time there were several other mature students there. He got a Certificate in Handicraft and Science Technology, as it was then termed, and went back to college for a further year, this time living in college because the year's learning was intensive: previously he and his family travelled up and down to his home town at weekends and lived in a house near the college, an operation which was expensive, and financed from the sale of the family business.

Gary began teaching at a school in his own town. He did not find it difficult to get a job, unlike many teachers in arts subjects. He estimates he is just as well off financially, and has *more* security than if he had stayed within the 'safety' of the family business.

In his case, breaking out of the family pressures trap cost a lot of money. He had to subsidise himself at the rate of several thousands of pounds a year for four years. If this had not been possible, he maintains he could have lived on a grant, by not travelling at weekends, giving up the house in his home locality while he was at college, and going without holidays.

I put to Gary the same question that I put to Stewart: *why* was the business he had entered because of the family pressures trap unsuitable for him?

> 'Perhaps from the point of view of business I have one basic disadvantage,' he said. 'I value the job more than the price which is on it. And I would very often take on jobs on this basis – because I was interested in them. I was interested in the design aspect. I found it absorbing and challenging and I needed this – whereas the sort of jobs which are challenging are not necessarily very rewarding financially. The jobs which are rewarding financially are the run-of-the-mill, boring jobs. Unfortunately, I was in the position to exercise the choice. I tended to gravitate towards the interesting things rather than the highly lucrative jobs.'

In other words, Gary's intellectual curiosity was always more important to him than profit. This factor – as potent a one as Stewart's ability to fight for others harder than for himself – should have been spotted from the first. It should have been forseen that it would bar him from a commercial career. It should have sent him towards the academic career he himself specifically wanted. The family pressures trap tends to ignore such personal factors; even to be unaware that they exist.

This can cause considerable bloody-mindedness in its victims. It is healthy symptom: the earlier it appears, the better. In the twenties, it can lead to action; by the forties it is likely to drain away all energy and undermine action.

The creatively bloody-minded

In Walter, the secretary of an artistes' charity (a position he might not have had but for his bloody-mindedness), rebelliousness appeared by the age of sixteen, but did not come into productive focus until some years later.

Walter has all the manners, accents and problems of the upper middle class man in an age where these are not common, or even desired, currency. His father is in the City of London, as was *his* father. He went to a private preparatory school, and then on to public school.

He was 31 at the time of our interview, and settled in a job which suited him, its modest salary augmented by a private income. At sixteen, when he left public school with eight O levels but no A levels, the future was cloudy, both to him and his parents, who plainly did not know what to make of him.

> 'I left public school somewhat earlier than had been expected,' he told me at his elegant flat. 'I didn't enjoy public school. I don't think I contributed very much to the school and I don't think I gained very much from it, although I was school librarian for two or three years. The library was my principal interest. I think I didn't get the best out of my chances because I thought my parents expected a lot from me, and I had a stubborn feeling that I wasn't going to exercise my talents until I was able to do so by myself.'

He went to a crammer, 'a very curious, somewhat Dickensian place,' where he got some A levels. Then he articled himself to a firm of chartered accountants, on the suggestion of his family. The family pressures trap was closing in on him.

After four years in articles, he was expected to pass the accountancy examinations. He did not. He did not complete the last examination. He drifted into a series of temporary accountancy jobs for a year, as a self-employed person acting through an agency.

His own explanation showed a greater degree of self-awareness than is possessed by many others who submit to the family pressures trap for longer than he did.

> 'I think I didn't continue in articles until I had got qualifications because I realised that my inability to pass the final examination was not due to any lack of application to my studies, but to a *refusal* actually to do the work when I sat the examination. I sat there and submitted blank papers with my name written neatly on the top and little else. I think I was being stupidly obstinate as I didn't really want to become an accountant.'

After the year of temporary accountancy work, he was approached by friends who owned a shop. He went to work for them as accountant and administrator, with the vague possibility of a partnership in due course. But after two years in the shop, it became clear that the partnership was not going to materialise.

Why not? 'I think because there was a difference in character between the man who was running it and myself. He and I didn't always see eye-to-eye on how the business should be run. I think he saw himself as a trader to whom any detailed administration was a time-wasting nuisance, whereas I saw myself as someone who was trying to keep the administration side under control.'

He worked for eighteen months with a finance house, giving administrative back-up to booming insurance sales; but got out when the cracks were beginning to appear in the boom of the 1970s. Just as he was thinking he must do something else in the City of London, and feeling rather resentful about it, he saw an advertisement in *The Times* for a course run by the Arts Council of Great Britain for administrators in the field of arts.

> 'I decided to go along to the Arts Council and see what it was all about,' said Walter. 'They gave me an application form and a prospectus of the course, which was the Polytechnic in Central London, and said, "By the way, applications close tomorrow." So I sat down there and then in the room and wrote out the application form, filled in the names of a couple of referees and had my photograph taken in Bond Street Underground Station and submitted my application. They chose me for a place on the course. It was done on the spur of the moment, really. I don't think there was anything carefully planned.'

Walter was beginning to escape, via his bloody-mindedness, from the family pressures trap. There were 16 on the course, chosen from 650 applicants.

His training involved a year's course, both classwork and external fieldwork, leading to a diploma in administration of the arts. Walter's external work included secondment to a regional arts association and to an art gallery outside London.

His bloody-mindedness was now waning as he gravitated towards the sorts of activity that really interested him. He enjoyed both his secondments. Both the regional arts association and the art gallery offered him jobs.

> 'I rather enjoyed both my secondments to these organisations and learned a lot more from secondments than I did from classwork. The courses seemed to be orientated towards people who were exponents of the arts trying to become administrators, rather than administrators who were trying to understand something about the arts. I learned a lot from my fellow students about the arts and certainly developed an interest in opera and music which I hadn't had before.'

This side of his nature, which was to pave the way to his

later job with the charity, might well not have emerged at all but for his resistance to accepting the dictates of family expectation. Now it had come to the surface, he began looking for jobs in administration at art galleries.

In fact, the charity knew he was looking for a job – through its contacts with the Arts Council – and wrote to him. He joined as an accountant. After four months he was offered the job of secretary, effectively in charge of the charity, on the retirement of the then secretary at the age of 65.

I asked Walter if he felt as bloody-minded now as he did when he was in accountancy, though the question was already answered in his demeanour.

> 'I don't feel bloody-minded at all, not in the slightest. I find it difficult to pin down why. I think it is the feeling of working for an organisation where I am in charge. I am reporting to a committee, but the day-to-day decisions are my responsibility. If it doesn't work it is my fault, it is nobody else's. I have got to get on and do it. I think it is the sense that I am leading a team of people who have an interest in view.'

What, then, had unfitted Walter for pure accountancy in the City of London?

> 'I think I now have the feeling that one is doing something that is not sterile, that one is not just making money for the sake of it. I am not just juggling with figures for the sake of the balance sheet. At the end of the day, someone has a roof over their head, or, less dramatically than that, a meal where they wouldn't otherwise have had one.'

In Walter's case, the personality characteristics of both Stewart and Gary came into play: desire to help other people and lack of interest in making money as such.

Walter's salary was about one half of what he might be earning if he had stayed in the City. It is true that a private income helps to heal such wounds, but he protested that he had never had regrets about the money.

> 'But I think that it has affected the way I look at my friends, especially the way I look on friends who continued in the City. Rightly or wrongly, I find it more difficult to understand the way they think about some problems and some of the aspects of life today. I mean, did I have a social conscience before I left the City or did I develop a social conscience as the result of working for a charity? I don't know . . . I think that, of my friends who have remained in the City, some regard me with a feeling that I never did make the best of my potential as an accountant or a businessman, mixed with a degree of envy that I have control over my own future and destiny in a way they don't.'

Walter believes that if at first he was in rebellion against his middle class parents, it was not in a conventional way: he did not 'drop out' or take drugs or wear his hair long.

> 'Instead, I think my rebellion probably manifested itself in failing to meet the expectations my family had for me. That was successful public school, university, leading to the Civil Service or to a lucrative profession like the law or accountancy. I think my mother certainly felt that if I am happy, then I must be doing the right thing. But my father, I think, was more sceptical, more doubtful about my change of career. I think he feels that one day I may want to go back to the City and won't be able to. I don't share that view. I feel that if after five years or so with the charity – if I have made a success of it – I want to go back into business, that five years' service for others would not prejudice

> my application to go back into business, although obviously I would find it difficult to go back specialising in tax work, for instance.'

I was interested to know whether his drop in sheer earning capacity had left him with a feeling of partial failure.

> 'No. The feeling of failure was much stronger when I was in the City. Because then I could see young men of my own age who had really made millions by the age of thirty; and I knew that I was not of that calibre.'

That is the pain the family pressures trap inflicts on its victims at worst: the feeling of playing in the wrong league, and so playing badly. Not all cases are so severe. Some people decide in middle age that family pressures have pushed them into a position which is quite tolerable, or even actively satisfying, but which leaves some sort of gap.

Such gaps, more minor, are best filled with palliatives in occupation rather than a complete break with the past.

The part-time curate

Hugh did not regard himself as a victim of family pressures. When I met him he was chairman of a merchant banking group in the City of London, not in the least bloody-minded about his job and very successful at it. He was also a part-time curate, at a salary of precisely one peppercorn a year.

The modification in his life was not predictable. I found, when I went to his sparse and ruthlessly neat office in the City of London, the sort of man who would gravitate to some sort of position of authority in any vocation requiring rugged self-projection. It would not have been surprising had he been a bishop; it was surprising to find him a part-time curate at a salary that was a mere formality and of no value, especially when paid in four equal quarterly instalments (a quarter peppercorn per three months).

I asked him how he had come into merchant banking in the first place.

> 'Oh, heavens above, a perfectly ordinary answer. It was a very small family firm after the war. In those days if one had a family firm there was a lot to be said for going into one. I am against it now: I don't think it is so relevant in the extremely professional circumstances in which we live. But it seemed, at the time, the obvious thing to do. I went into it for no better reason than that.'

He was 22. He had just come out of the Army. He had had no experience of civilian working life and felt 'very lost'. He worked at a news agency for nine months because he thought it might be fun. Then he thought about the Church, but decided that the time did not *feel* right for it.

> 'I was aware that I was too immature. I was *very* immature. I recognised that, I think. I dismissed the thought of the Church because I felt that even if it was right for me, at that stage I was too immature for it. I put it behind me absolutely at that stage, not merely temporarily.'

The leanings towards the Church returned. Original leanings often do return in people who have dismissed them for 'common-sense' reasons, only to find that some impulses go deeper than common-sense.

> 'We are dealing here with something that is outside

> the rational and quite definitely in the realm of the spiritual,' he tried to explain. 'There was no suggestion at all of my sitting down and saying to myself, "I am in such-and-such a position now and I reckon that the job here is OK up to a point but I miss out on this, this, and this and I am going to look elsewhere." No question of that at all.'

The family trap, in his case, was one of the gentlest; and he did not really resent its teeth. But in his forties he went through a period of 'rethinking what life is really all about'.

> 'One goes through a period of thinking in one's late teens and early twenties. Then you get on with the job, get to the next rung of the ladder, marry and set up a home and have children. Then afterwards, in the mid-forties, one can sit there and recognise that life is not infinite, as it seems in one's early twenties, and that death is coming at some point. And one really says, "Look, what's the point of it all? What am I doing? Where am I going to go?" '

His perplexity was increased by what he saw as a general malaise in the society around him. It seemed to him that a lot of mankind was getting into an awful muddle, a not uncommon feeling in men in their forties who sit down and think hard. Inflation was then getting worse. The economic situation was declining. Now, in his mid-forties, he found that people had less respect for Parliament as a whole.

To him, the social scene was deteriorating. The increase in permissiveness and violence made him ask himself where mankind was going. It also made him ask himself: 'Can I, a puny unit in the sea of mankind, do anything? If so, where do I apply my shoulder and the very, very small amount of weight I have got?'

It is not uncommon for successful men to reach a

plateau in their careers and then find something wanting in mankind. He knew that. But in Hugh's case there seemed objective reasons for the point of view. He remembers thinking that he had a choice. It was between doing something in the humanistic area (perhaps as a probation worker or social worker in his spare time) and exploring the spiritual area.

> 'In this, I draw a total distinction between the spiritual power and Christianity and anything to do with spiritualism. Where the Christian gospel is taught straight, without pulling punches, it brings people fulfilment and a sense of inner peace and joy which all of us long for and which is lacking otherwise. But I know that in the way I am now describing it, it sounds as if it were a purely rational decision. One must remember the fact that Christianity is of little use unless one is aware of Christ as a living person to whom the ordinary human being like myself, you, or anybody else, can relate and have a living relationship with.'

Sceptics may see the self-drawn picture of Hugh, at this stage in his development, as being of a man lonely on the pinnacle of worldly success and in need of companionship. Such may or may not be the explanation: it is impossible to penetrate someone else's skull. In the last resort, it does not much matter. Whether a person having middle-aged doubts is rationalising or not does *not* remove the central point that there is an impetus of some kind to be acted on.

In any case, Hugh was still not at the pinnacle of his success. He was then a director of the firm, but not yet its chairman. He still had rungs to climb. He would not have been human if he had not wondered how the resurgence of his feelings towards the Church would affect his City work, which he did not intend to give up. Did it affect his attitude to his City work?

> 'I can only answer that by quoting the words of an extremely wise old woman in Norfolk who said to me shortly before I was finally ordained, "You know, you will find each job will help the other." I have found that to be true.'

As a priest, he said, it had been of enormous help to be a practical businessman. He found it of great help to be able to say in the course of a sermon, 'Well, I am in the City and I run a group with eight or nine hundred other people and I have to concern myself with something that is practical.' He remembered saying to a young insurance broker:

> ' "I reject everything in Christianity that I don't regard as practical for a middle-aged, reasonably successful business executive to accept." But in practice the tougher I am about applying this test, the *more* I find I believe. This is because the Gospel is true.'

Such a view of Christianity may be too robust for some tastes. It appears to have served Hugh well in his own benefice as a part-time curate, just as his practicality served him well in actually realising his leanings towards the Church. He approached it rather as he might approach any other major decision, resisting it until he was certain. He had the thought; then he edged away from it. Then he edged towards it again, and so on. He was fairly used to making decisions alone.

He looked rather incredulous when I asked him whether he had discussed it with his friends, perhaps at the golf club: 'I discussed it with my wife, who was wonderful, and the children, too. But otherwise, no. Why should I? It is a matter between me and the Almighty.'

He said he had nothing against people who used other people as sounding boards for such decisions. He thought it might be extremely wise and practical. But in the final analysis one had to *take the responsibility for one's own life*. Someone had once told him that, if one was on the brink of a big decision, one should ask everyone's advice and then make up one's own mind.

'I just skipped the first stage,' said Hugh.

He became a part-time curate by going to the Southwark Ordination Course, arranged by the Bishop of Southwark for people who wished to earn their living and train for either full-time or part-time ordination simultaneously.

Many men on the course did not decide until the last few months whether they were going to be full-time or part-time. In his own case, he was fairly certain that he would stay with his City job, using the one to cross-fertilise the other.

The course entailed a fortnight's residential study in the summer of each year; one weekend a month throughout the winter months and two evenings a week, for eight or nine months of the year, at the Chapter House outside London Bridge. In addition, there was a lot of reading and essay writing to be done privately.

> 'Fair comment,' said Hugh when I suggested to him that there might have been a conflict of interest while he was studying. 'I was working, then, a good sixty-hour week in the City, not all in the office. I worked in the train and took work home with me at the weekends. I think it is wrong for anyone to sacrifice their growing children and I had time for them. I can only say that Southwark were extremely understanding and recognised that I couldn't give the same amount of time as a man who, perhaps, worked from nine to five and didn't have any children. My two children were then in their teens. They were very enthusiastic about it. But, particularly at that age, children must feel their parents have got time for them. I certainly did not give as much as ten hours a week to the course. Both my wife and I were

> sad at the separation over the weekends and it definitely got in the way of one's social life, which ceased to exist – seeing friends at home and so on. Otherwise there was no psychological price. I don't think you feel the strain if you know what you are doing is right. I think that is one of the facts of life. People often ask me how I manage to do both jobs even now. I do make a point about the help of one's wife. This has been vital to me. I couldn't possibly cope without my wife's total support. But otherwise, if you are absolutely certain within you that what you are doing is right, then you are given the strength to do it.'

Hugh admitted only to being frustrated in the first three years of his life in the City of London.

> 'My first three years, I rebelled the whole time . . . One was an energetic young bloke and one was not able to get any satisfaction at all. Everyone was awfully *nice* to me, but . . . I had held positions of responsibility at school and I had been an officer in the Army, and a clerk's job was very dreary. I am well aware of the frustrations some people can experience in their work.'

As one who had been passingly frustrated, what would his advice be to a stockbroker who, perhaps because he was caught in the family pressures trap, was permanently unfulfilled in his work?

> 'You have to start where someone *is* at the moment,' said Hugh. 'To the stockbroker unfulfilled in his work, the answer is that he needs to commit his whole life in love and trust in Our Lord. He needs to stop fighting and to submit – not submit to the Stock Exchange, but to submit to Our Lord who will, if He is allowed to, lead him and either help him to

> adjust if it is His will that he stay there, or lead him out of it in due course – and when he is ready for it and not before. This view will sound desperately trite, but it is true.'

The misplaced girl

The desire to see a son or daughter in the family business, on the practical argument that his or her presence is 'badly needed' for the good of the business, may be one of the most powerful of family pressure traps. It is not the only one. Parental vanity can be almost as dangerous a snare if it takes the form of wishing the child to follow the same line of business or vocation as the parent, even if not in the same organisation.

The family pressures trap exerted on Pamela was a many-sided one. She was born in the North, the middle one of three girls. There was no boy in the family. Looking back, she believed she was unconsciously given that role by her parents. A certain briskness of manner and adrenal energy, when I interviewed her at her present home in the South, might indicate that she was still trying to fulfil it. As she was so evidently a feminine and sexually attractive woman, such a posture could not be held without strain.

As a young girl, the strain was compounded. From the age of five, she wanted to be a doctor.

> 'I was dissuaded,' she said. 'I think, in perfectly good faith, my parents thought it was not a suitable career for a woman at that time. I was gently steered into chemistry.'

The steering may have been gentle. It was not disinterested. Her father was a PhD in chemistry. Her mother had a degree in biology and chemistry; and *her* father had a degree in chemistry, and taught maths. Any stranger, looking dispassionately at Pamela, would quickly detect a strong desire to care for people. It was not detected by her conscientious parents: one more illustration of the fact that academic cleverness does not necessarily go proportionately hand in hand with human perception.

It took some persuasion to get Pamela to talk about her parents' attitude; then she explained that she could do so only because both her parents were now dead. It is not unusual for the parental pressures trap to extend to imposing a vow of silence on its victims, who feel disloyal if they openly express what every human being is entitled to express: the signs of satisfaction or dissatisfaction with the way one is earning one's daily bread.

Even now they were dead, Pamela still felt some compulsion to defend their mistake as vigorously as possible.

> 'My best subject at school was probably maths. Probably it still is. I never took maths seriously, because it was a game – so easy. But there was one stage at the grammar school I attended when I did tell the maths master that I wanted to do maths and not chemistry. And he very strongly dissuaded me. I think this was probably due to his respect for my father.'

Instead of following her own sense of vocation, she went to university and took a degree in chemistry. She graduated at the age of twenty, the only girl in her year. Then she did four years in industrial research, first in agriculture and then in the confectionery industry.

> 'I was never particularly happy in industry,' she said. 'I still loved my subject, but being a woman was an enormous disadvantage in industry. I felt that,

whatever I did, the men I was working with – who might have fewer qualifications and do less work – would automatically get the promotion and the bigger salaries.I didn't eat with the executive staff. I ate with the office staff, although I was salaried staff. Pinpricks. This would be when I was aged between 20 and 24. I had my first son just before I was 25. I worked until a couple of months before he was born.'

At this point, the family pressures trap worked in an additional way. Her parents persuaded her not to go on working – 'nice women *didn't*'.

'They didn't want me to go on working at all, not after I was married,' she said. 'The script I got as a child – which I think my sister got as well – was that you educate women because they might be widowed and they might be divorced. Therefore they have to have a career to fall back on. But once they are married, they don't work, they give up everything. Which of course, is what my mother did, also being a graduate.'

Still Pamela did not feel active dissatisfaction with her life. It began when her husband took a job in Australia at the age of thirty. He moved because he would have had to wait at least another ten years for such a job in Britain. She herself was not working.

'In Australia,' she said, 'I found the position of a woman of my social class – and I think social class is highly relevant to Australia, although they call it a classless society – was absolutely insupportable. Women had no freedom, they had no respect. As I got to know Australian women, which took several years, the thing they most commonly said to me was, "You are so lucky, your husband treats you as an equal." This was rare. I *was* lucky – my husband did treat me as an equal. But I found that when I went into shops and was served by a man, he treated me as if I were intellectually an imbecile. Which is not what I am used to – or, indeed, what I am . . . It was after our fourth child was born that I began to think again about work. I looked into the field of chemistry, and there was virtually nothing there. I could have done routine analytical work. But so much of the chemical industry of Australia was overseas-owned and all the research was done overseas. And, really, no one was interested in a married woman. A married woman would stop work, and was automatically a vegetable.'

Pamela then did what many people who successfully change careers in middle-age manage to do. She converted her misfortune into her fortune. She found herself one evening ringing up a cousin of her husband's, a professor at Monash University, and saying to him: 'I want to do medicine. What can I do about it?' She had not even discussed it with her husband.

She was then 31. She was invited for interview at Monash, the Australian second university, started primarily to produce a medical school to augment Melbourne's. She was interviewed by the secretary of the faculty of medicine. He told her:

> 'To be perfectly frank, I interviewed you as a matter of courtesy, to gently dissuade you. I assumed you had only matriculation, which is the Australian university entrance, and nothing since then. As you have a degree and particularly a science degree, we are not going to dismiss you. Yes, we will be interested.'

At Monash, she did the second and third years of the medical course, then started clinical work. At this point her husband got another job back in England. She had to give up the course. She was 36. She could only hope that a British university would accommodate her. She contacted Oxford and several of the London medical schools on her return and (perhaps fortunately) they made her angry. Anger is a positive and combative emotion.

> 'I hit bureaucracy,' she said. 'They even began to get worried about whether I had matriculation maths. With a degree in chemistry, they got terribly worried about whether I had matriculation maths! You can't do *anything* in a British university without matriculation maths. I had arranged an interview with the University of London. I travelled down from Newcastle, where I was staying at the time. When I arrived, the gates were barred. They had been having one of their student uprisings at the London School of Economics. At first, I was refused entry altogether. It wasn't until I got very, very angry that they went to find the woman who was supposed to be interviewing me and brought me down to the barred gates to meet me and take me in. And really all this was about whether I had matriculation maths. At this stage I parcelled up my birth certificate and my marriage certificate, every certificate I could find, and thought, "Surely these will convince them". Which they seem to have done . . . But they just didn't want to know.'

Nor did Oxford. It was thought that travelling every day from Amersham, where they were then living, would be too much for her. It was a forty-minute drive.

It was at this point that Pamela ostensibly gave up. She remembered using her medical student jackets for painting the house. Then, fortunately or with unconscious shrewdness about how to stage-manage herself, she got angry again. She began to ask questions, and wrote to a lot more London medical schools. Eventually she got a letter from the secretary of one of the schools which does accept late entrants. She was finally admitted at the age of 38, having lost two years.

A junior hospital doctor involved in psychiatry when I interviewed her, she was able to say self-comfortingly that because she was older, she had more authority than if she had started medicine younger.

> 'Looking back, I have no regrets that I did not study medicine at eighteen. I don't think I could have coped then with the work I did later. I don't think I wasted the years when my parent's influence pushed me away from medicine. What I did in them has made me a better psychiatrist. It was an experience that I could not possibly have got if I had been in medicine at the time. But I do, I think, possibly regret the soul-searching that coming late into medicine caused me. And again, this is my upbringing, about what women did do and didn't do. I think my mother was probably exceptionally rigid in this. Having started studying in Australia, I wondered what my parents' attitude would be when I told them. I think I looked upon that with a great deal of apprehension: how they would react. I didn't really get a reaction until I came back to England. My mother was dead by then. And my father was absolutely delighted at what I had done. My father told me that *his* father had wanted him to be a doctor and he had never felt he could face medicine and, in the event, a PhD was the best he could offer his father. He said, "If only your grandfather could see you now, how happy he would be."'

And so the family pressures trap goes on its circular way, wasting the time of those who succumb to it and wasting the energy of those who fight it. The moral is clear. The family pressures trap is difficult to escape, but *it is* well worth the struggle, including the struggle of *not* passing it on to one's own children.

CHAPTER THREE: PATHS TO GIVING

Dick, an ex-public schoolboy with an admitted social inferiority complex when he was still an electrical engineer, made one stipulation when he and his wife opened an old people's home. He would certainly do the administration. He would certainly handle the business side. He would do the repair jobs if necessary. But his wife, Rachel, not he, would have to do the nursing of the residents. He couldn't see himself fetching bed pans.

In practice, he found he became drawn, willingly and rewardingly, into the nursing of the old people. He began to like the *giving* of himself that it entailed. His social sense of inferiority largely disappeared. It was based, he had come to think, not merely on his resentment of a manual job after his public school education, but on the feeling that it was not an avenue through which he could *give* to his fellow humans.

> 'I think I consciously came to want a job with more giving to it,' said Dick, a soft-featured man with a quiet voice and eyes that could easily register a wound. 'I am too soft, really, to be a hard-faced industrial foreman, which is what I was supposed to be, I suppose, when I worked for the Electricity Board. I am too soft with people. People tried to take advantage of me. People think, "A soft story, and it will be swallowed." It wasn't, but people would try it. Then the thought suddenly struck me one day, "God, I have another twenty-odd years of this – I

will never do it!" When we first opened the old people's home, we were working twenty hours a day, for about six months. I have done that in the electricity industry; I have worked three days solid for the electricity industry. I would think to myself, "I am doing it for the consumer," in the early days, though I didn't particularly like the job. It was appreciated. Now it wouldn't be.'

No one who comes to feel, in his middle life, that money is no longer an adequate incentive need feel alone. There may be social workers or doctors who have become financiers in middle life; but if so I did not get to hear about them. The main traffic is not usually in that direction, even though a financier may earn several times more than a doctor or social worker. It is far more likely that in middle life the financier will seek to become a social worker, or wish he were one. The main traffic flows in this direction.

Why? Because, if there is a career change in middle life, it is quite commonly towards *giving* more rather than *taking* more.

Cynics may say the reason is that the 'giving' jobs are easier to get because they are often ill-paid. It is an insufficient explanation. The impression I got after talking to people who have made the move was that, with greater maturity, there comes a realisation that deep satisfaction in life stems from giving rather than taking; of being used *by* others rather than using others. This is not a pious cliché. It is a practical fact of rewarding living, confirmed by Dick and many other people who have successfully changed jobs.

A direct act of giving, noticed as such, is obviously necessary to people of Dick's temperament: gentle and self-doubting. But such a man may find direct human contact paradoxically frightening at first. He may dislike parts of his personality, previously unexplored, being subjected to sudden scrutiny.

'When Dick first came in with me, he said, "I will do anything you want me to, but I don't want to get involved with the patients too much. I will do all the business side",' said his wife Rachel, who had herself worked for an old people's home in which she (revealingly) felt that the guests were not getting enough kindness and attention for their money. 'So I was left entirely to get on with the nursing side and with the patients. But he suddenly found that he became involved. A little bit more and then a little bit more. Now he does no end of things for the patients. He will shave them and all that sort of thing. You find yourself doing all sorts of things you didn't realise you could do, don't you?'

'Yes,' said Dick, 'you never know what you can do until you try. I don't mind doing it. I am a happier person. I used to do the garden, and people thought I was the gardener, but I found I didn't mind, because I knew I wasn't. My pride was coming back.'

One of the facets of Dick's gentleness that stood out was that the response of other people was especially important to him. He himself said he thought it might be a form of 'selfishness'; but he said it in a way that showed he was hoping for a denial. *All* desire for satisfaction can be labelled as 'selfish' in one sense: but not meaningfully. If *constructive* satisfaction is 'selfish', then another word must be found for unconstructive or anti-social satisfaction. I assured Dick that I did not regard his attitude as selfish.

He then spoke more freely of the nature of the satisfaction he got from his new life, which he took on at the age of 45.

'You can see a person come in here,' he said, 'a relative of an old person, and they are at their wit's end. They don't know what to do. They are almost in tears. They say, "What shall I do? I can't cope with Mum, I can't cope with Dad. They are driving me crazy. My husband is putting up with it as best he can, but we are continually rowing. Can you help us?" And Rachel will say: "Yes, we can." The relief that shows on a person's face! They go away. Their mother or father will come in here. After three or four weeks the old person who is staying here will look far better. The daughter will come in to see her parent, and she is a totally different person, too. You think to yourself, "Oh well, I have made someone happy." In this day and age, it is swimming against the current, which is satisfying. It is satisfying because, if everyone else is trying to climb up on someone else's back, you are moving against the stream. Kindness is a very rare commodity, isn't it? Looking back on my life, I think this was the purpose for which we were meant. I have been on both sides of the fence.'

The fence Dick meant was the social fence. His concept of it, before he took to the path of giving through his old people's home, crippled his happiness and (even more importantly) his self-respect.

He had been the prisoner of his own background. He was the son of parents who were 'Victorian' in their attitudes: his father was also in electrical engineering, and wanted his son to have a 'safe' job. Dick was evacuated to the North during the war, where he went to a grammar school. Then he came back to a public school in his home area. He was a weekly boarder. Most of his fellow pupils were the sons of professional people and were bound for professional careers.His parents had strict ideas of proper etiquette. They always used laundered linen napkins – unlike their neighbours. Dick's 21st birthday present from his parents was a dinner jacket.

Every fact of Dick's life – except the central one of the

job he was going to take with the Electricity Board – conditioned him to expect for himself the situation of a gentleman. The reality was conditioned by the fact he was a cable jointer, a man who worked in holes in the street.

> 'I was taking an electrical engineering course which, on reflection, was a waste. I was just not cut out for it. I was not particularly good at maths, and all engineering is maths. Being at a grammar school in those days and being at a boarding school, you are on one side of the social fence. Then you suddenly find yourself completely on the other. This cable-jointing involved working on underground cables in the road, in the main street – here, there and everywhere. And jumping from one side of the fence to the other is quite a step. My pride was hurt. When you are young, and you think you are God's gift to the world . . . Well, my pride was hurt, it really was. Lots of my school friends, lots of people I knew, came along as I was working in the road. They were manager of this that or the other, or professional people – I think one of them is now a solicitor and another a chartered accountant – and they saw you stuck down a hole in the road. I admit I used to look away because I was ashamed of myself.'

A *giving* sort of job gave Dick a healthier sort of perspective on his past experience, ending his resentment: 'On reflection, it has all helped me to understand people. I can see now it has served a purpose.'

Looking back on Dick's reactions to his job in electrical engineering, it is easy to see that the increasingly selfish (as he saw it) nature of his work as an Organisation Man was the very factor which was helping him to do something decisive. This, he admitted, he always tended to find difficult.

He was forty when he seriously thought of making a change. He had been made distribution foreman, which meant he had an office job, with over a dozen men in his charge, under the general control of an engineer.

> 'The whole thing got so ridiculous. Reorganisation and modern management, and work study and method study, were starting to come in. Trades unions were involved in it. People would find any excuse not to do anything, and be highly delighted in doing so. Every obstacle was put in the way of doing something. You find yourself practising preventive things, not constructive ones. All you find yourself doing is working to keep your nose clean. Keep your plate clear, so there are no come-backs on you. The job is secondary. All you are doing, really, is keeping yourself out of trouble, which is wrong. If anything went wrong, it was always: "Whose fault is it? Who is to blame? Who can we hang this on?" I am not a person like that. All right, if someone makes a *deliberate* mistake, yes. But if not – well, anybody can make a mistake and if anybody accepts it, then that is fair enough. There was empire-building. Everybody would cut your throat as soon as look at you. The days when the consumer was the number one priority had gone. It just didn't matter.'

Difficulty in imposing discipline may or may not be the responsibility of the organisation employing the potential disciplinarian: some who do it successfully might say that Dick was rationalising his own temperamental short-comings. His view that the consumer did not count any more might also be challenged by others who stayed in his particular industry. But whether Dick was being objective or subjective does not really matter: the very fact that rationalisations for unease are *sought* proves the unease exists. If a hundred people thought it was possible to do a constructive job in the electricity industry, it would not in the least alter the fact that Dick's disaffection was quite real *as it affected himself*. It was not *his* idea of a 'giving' job. He had to find one which was.

Having found it, Dick also found a sense of 'having built something', which a thousand re-laid cables would not have given him.

> 'You get satisfaction in this job, you really do,' he said. 'I am contented. This is what life is about – you are alright if you have got peace of mind and contentment. I think I have got self-respect back again. I feel as if now I have achieved something from what – way back in my early days – I was taught, and from what I was meant to do and capable of doing. We have built something. I am a great family man, I believe in families and the continuation of families, family heirlooms and suchlike. I love my parents dearly, and that is the reason we called the home after them. My boys are called after my mother's maiden name . . . Looking back on my life, I think I do regret the wasted years. I should have made the change earlier. But now I can see a reason for it. I have mixed with the humblest of the humblest and I can talk to them. Who was it who said, "When you can walk with kings and talk with beggars, you are a man, my son"? I feel I have done this with my schooling and with my days at the Electricity Board. I feel that I have spanned the whole of society, and this I am grateful for.'

Dick got out of a job he had always disliked by steady attention to *one idea which his general situation had made real*.

His wife had always been interested in old people, and had worked at old people's homes. He talked about the prospect of opening one for themselves for three years; until he felt he would never actually get round to doing it. His fear of the unknown, of stepping out of a secure job, gradually waned before the familiarity of the 'new' idea. He rationalised his new thoughts as best he could on business lines. Wouldn't looking after old people be a 52-weeks-a-year paying proposition; whereas, say, keeping a boarding house would mean good business in the summer season and vacant rooms at other times? Was he a gambling sort of person? No, he wasn't. In that case, wasn't it more attractive, a surer bet, to be full 52 weeks of the year?

Then a local hotel came on the market. It was Rachel who saw the advertisement in the local newspaper. She recalled saying to her husband, 'My God, there is a fourteen-bedroomed hotel here and the price seems reasonable.' Dick said there was no harm in looking at it. They looked. Rachel said: 'We are going to have it, lock, stock and barrel.'

That left them with the financial problems to sort out. Here the banks proved helpful. Why? Because Dick and Rachel had a good banking record with them, and they could prove they were careful with money.

> 'We have done everything we could to make money,' said Rachel. 'Not scrabbling to make money. But if we saw an opportunity, we took it. We used to sell chickens ready-cooked, before all this frozen business started. I used to cook six at a time and people came to the door to buy them. We would make a profit out of that, so we had money in the bank. And we used to have bed and breakfast. We got bored one summer, when I was having my son, and we were living in an area of retired people. We decided to put up a bed and breakfast notice and within about an hour people were knocking on the door and I said to Dick, "This is marvellous. While we are asleep, we are earning money." Mind you, it was only 12s.6d. [62p.] a night for bed and breakfast but our rooms were being used. We did this for a whole summer and made quite a lot of money. Our beds were never empty. The next year I did bed and

breakfast *and* evening meal for double the price and we gradually made quite a lot – didn't we, Dick? And we kept it. And our house mortgage was nothing to worry about, because we put all we had got into it to start with, so we had no worries there, we were not paying out a lot of money in mortgage or anything like that. So we were quite nicely placed, and the bank realised it.'

This attempt at acquiring an hotel did not come off. The owners had another offer, which they accepted just as Dick and Rachel were about to sign the contract. 'We were so upset, we felt we had been kicked in the stomach, didn't we, Dick? said Rachel. 'We felt it was a dreadful thing.'

It did not dim their determination. In fact it demonstrated the fact that an abortive experience in job-changing can provide both a boost to the adrenalin and experience which will be valuable later.

When Dick and Rachel were explaining their disappointment at a friend's house, the friend said she knew a woman who wanted to sell her fine old house 'if it was to somebody I know.' Dick and Rachel decided it would be ideal for them. All they then had to do was tell the bank to re-activate the plans already agreed for the hotel: basically to supply working capital, while the couple bought the house with their savings and a private loan.

For Dick, it was the end of the chief problem which had cramped his personality and happiness.

He said that he was now not aware of his former feelings of social inferiority:

'I am still not a doctor or a lawyer, but I am somebody in the community. I am not ashamed of what I am doing, I am not ashamed of being a failure any more. I was ashamed of myself for a long, long time. That gnawed at me over the years. Now it doesn't any more. I am happy here in the home. I am

> basically a home person. I feel I am doing something in life, something that will go on when I am no more. My wife and I will have left something in the world. We will say, "Well, we have done something, we have left something." And so it is all worthwhile in the end, isn't it?'

This last sentiment was revealing. Discussion with a high proportion of job changers I interviewed indicated clearly that not only is rationalising discontent a sign that the job is wrong; rationalising *all past experience as useful* is a sign that the new job is right for the person concerned.

The involuntary benefactor

Malcolm failed his chartered accountancy examinations and settled for a job in the administration of a professional institute. When it was merged with others, he was not offered a job in the newly-created body. Instead it was suggested that he become secretary of the joint charity covering the three organisations which were merging. At first, Malcolm did not like the idea of the change.

> 'The merger was undoubtedly in the best interests of the professions concerned. But it left me feeling very worried. I felt that, coming into a charity, I was not going to have as much responsibility as I had had being finance officer of a big institution, dealing not only with finance and investments but also with buildings. I had really been office manager, staff manager, the whole lot. I felt very worried, too, over the question of how far one could go in a charity, especially at that time, with more and more state benefits coming in. I did say at the time that I felt I was not going into such a senior position, although my full salary and pension rights were guaranteed. I did feel that I might be going into a little backwater.'

Such were the thoughts of conventional ambition. In an active man of 45 (who had always said that if he missed a single night's sleep, he would straightaway go to the doctor, because he would know that something was wrong) it was quite understandable. It was probably what any other man in his position, and in his state of good health, would have felt.

> 'In fact,' said Malcolm, 'the very opposite happened to what I had feared. Now I wouldn't have missed the move for anything. At first I was not conscious of a change of direction in my life. But as this work expanded, a lot of it in the form of advice on how people can take advantage of state benefits to which they are entitled, I realised that I was getting more and more into the intricacies of people. It makes a great difference and gives you a very different outlook on life. I find the human giving very rewarding. You get magnificent letters back from some people. We have a system whereby, if a person looks like becoming what we call a regular case, we have a personal interview, done by someone from headquarters. I do that or my social worker does it. Recently I went to see a widow whose husband had been killed in a car crash. She said to me, "It was absolutely marvellous the way you spoke to me on the telephone, and said that you, an absolute stranger to me, would speak to the building society and get me an option mortgage." She had only fifteen days to get it, as it happened, so acting promptly made a difference. It is things like that, when people say "Thank you" for what you do. It really does give you a great deal of . . . no, "pleasure" is not the right word, but satisfaction that you have been able to do something for someone. Obviously, as in anything else, you always get five per cent of people who are not grateful; that happens in any work, doesn't it? But some of the letters we get for gifts we send out

at Christmas, and things like that, are absolutely fantastic and written from the heart. I don't look upon it as being addressed to me only. As I have told my staff, "The only things we have to *sell* here are our public relations and our personal relations with beneficiaries." '

Malcolm, at 52, said he believed that, had he continued with his duties as a finance officer, he would by now be dreading Monday mornings and also experiencing a drop in his energies.

'I needed added stimulation to keep my energy levels up. Moving into a more human sphere of activity has given me that charge of energy. There is no question about it at all. On reflection, I wouldn't have missed the last seven years for anything. I couldn't have gone on with auditing all my life. I got out of that when I was 27, because it was too mechanical. It was rather the same with my second move, to charity administration. I gained because there was a greater element of helping people. I like people. They have never worried me. You can't like everybody, but I have never minded dealing with people. If I were a commercial traveller I would be dealing with people, but it would not be the same. The difference is the benevolent aspect.'

In saying this Malcolm was not, I decided, being carried away by rosy sentiment. He was not that kind of man. As a realist, he conceded (which few escapists and Peter Pans do) that his previous experience had not been a waste; because it could be used in his newer, more giving occupation. It is this blend of sentiment and realism that makes for the greatest success in changing over to a more altruistic career.

'No,' said Malcolm, 'I don't think that, even with

hindsight, I would have followed a different route at the age of sixteen, when I left school. I think that to be in charity work all one's life might be a bit taxing. I think I probably changed at the right time, as it happened. It is important that charities should have good and properly paid staff. I don't think I would have gone into the job in my twenties because the salaries were low. In those days so much was done by volunteers. These days you have got to have professionally-trained people, albeit in small numbers. One of the good things, coming in as I did, and having had audit and administration experience, was that I could bring both of these skills into a charity. I think this is important. Financial expertise is very important in a charity. One of the things people start shouting about is the administrative expense of a charity fund, in relation to whatever you may make from donations. This is where financial expertise comes in. Everyone who comes into a charity should bring some skill in with them.'

Involving the wife

Several people I interviewed after they had changed jobs said vaguely that they were looking for more 'interesting' jobs. When their motives were analysed in more detail, 'more interesting' usually meant more giving and often meant, also, more interesting *to their wives* as well as themselves.

It was so in the case of Kenneth. When I saw him he was general secretary of a charity that provides shelter for old people, having been previously with a giant oil firm as a research physicist and personnel executive.

He made his major change at the age of fifty. He started off with the oil firm in basic research, had a spell in London while he took a part-time degree, then went into deeper research laboratories. He did this until a reorganisation, when he was offered a job on the junior personnel side.

> 'I suppose that does suggest that I was not totally involved in the sheer physics side and that I wanted something more to do with people,' said Kenneth. 'And my wife-to-be, as she was in those days, had worked with an organisation connected with personnel management. It sounded very interesting to me. Anyhow, with the reorganisation, the company remembered my interest in personnel work over the years and offered me a job. I was chucked in at the deep end, with no training. It meant recruiting junior staff, looking after junior staff salaries, and developing contacts with things like schools. I found it was a very natural change.'

Kenneth said he did not think that, at this stage, the thought that he could do something even *more* different had entered his head.

> 'Except,' he said, 'that I have always been an advocate of change of career at, say, fifty. There is nothing magic about fifty. But before you got to the run-up to retirement, I always felt you had reached your peak. So why flog yourself in the last ten years on something that somebody else might do better? Why maintain yourself up there when everyone else was gunning for your job? That is the situation for most people.'

It is certainly the situation for people who feel, perhaps unconsciously, that they are ready for a different sort of working slot. In Kenneth's case, he believed that salaries should peak at fifty and then come down. He agreed that this would not be socially acceptable as a general rule, but pointed out that average human needs peaked at around fifty, when children were leaving home.

'You need more money earlier and less money after. It means you have to take a less responsible job, if you keep salary and job in line. So you take a less responsible job, but perhaps a more interesting one.'

In Kenneth's case, an 'interesting' job would be even more interesting if it could also involve his wife. This attitude is not unusual; it is at around the age of fifty that parents watch their children depart from home and begin to look with new eyes on what they both have in common, and sometimes, though not in Kenneth's case, whether it is enough to keep them together.

It was another reorganisation within the oil firm that nudged him towards a job he could share more with his wife, and which also involved some sort of outward giving.

'I had foreseen staying in personnel work with the company for the rest of my life,' said Kenneth. 'I expected that to be my career until age sixty, and I would then be retired in the automatic way. But eventually I knew that in three years' time the laboratories in which I worked were going to be shut. They were going to take the work somewhere else. So everybody, the staff of 450, had to leave those laboratories. Over a period of three years we had to find jobs for, say, 250 people – 150 were transferred and 50 disappeared off their own bat. That total experience of running down the laboratory, where *everybody* had to think about a change of career, was a tremendously challenging job and fairly satisfying because you could help people take the right attitude to it.'

During this process, Kenneth was presented with the fact that other people could, and did, completely change their occupations.

'You saw a research scientist becoming a Church of England parson, or something like that. In fact, they could change into almost anything. It was surprising what they could do when the need was there.'

The atmosphere encouraged Kenneth to be experimental in his thinking. He came across a newspaper advertisement, under a box number, which did not state the name of the employer, but which said the job was 'one of the most interesting and challenging in one of the Free Churches. Kenneth had been of the denomination all his life, and had been educated at one of its schools.

'I thought, "What are these people writing about?" I thought it was going to be at Notting Hill, or something like that. So I wrote a rather funny sort of letter, not very serious at all, saying in effect, "Look, what right have you to say you have the most challenging job? In fact, in three years' time, I will be leaving my present job and I want a job with old people if possible, something in which my wife can be interested and involved as well. If we have mutual ground, I will be interested in who you are, and perhaps we can have a chat?" Much to my surprise, a letter came back from this charity, and I had really no idea the advertisement was to do with old people. At any rate, they were interested to meet and talk to me. They said, "In three years' time, we will be pleased to have you." They didn't say exactly what the job was. They had thought there was personnel work in it: recruiting staff, looking after staff, that sort of thing. In practice, there was a change of organisation in between and I ended up as the general secretary. I knew that my salary would be very much lower: it would be less than half. It did not give me much pause for thought. I thought I had quite adequate means and my children were getting to the stage where they were likely to become gradually self-supporting. I could have stopped with the oil company, and my salary would have gone up. I was reasonably respected, so I don't doubt I would have had a satisfying post with prospects.'

Two factors helped clinch Kenneth's move. Both were concerned with aspects of giving.

The first was definitely that he saw in the new job something in which his wife could cooperate. He had a daughter in poor health, and it was a source of satisfaction to him that he had a job which helped his wife take her mind off this domestic problem.

> 'It gave her a practical outlet,' said Kenneth. 'She could come with me on some of my visits to old people's homes, while our daughter was being looked after, and so on. I think the fact that my wife could join me was the overriding thing in my decision to take this on.'

The second factor was that Kenneth saw in the new job a chance to respond to a *different degree of need* to the one to which he had had to respond as a personnel man for the oil company.

Among the old people, he said, there were many desperate situations where he could help, whereas in the commercial job, the situations were never desperate:

> 'There were some cases with which you had sympathy, but there was no desperation about it. Here we have people who desperately need your help *today*. Although we can't help that quickly, every now and again we can jump in and say, "Yes, we have facilities," or "We can bend the rules to help you now." That is the difference in the degree of need to which we can respond here, compared with industry, where I had a very comfortable life, despite the problems there – very comfortable and very easy. There is a religious or moral element in this job, which there wasn't in the old one, though I

did try to bring my moral side and my religious thinking into my personnel job. It was part of it. But it was perhaps more difficult to make it so apparent. It *feels* more apparent now, although it may or may not be. For instance, when a person was thwarted in their career at the oil company, we tried to help sort him out as to where he should go. You could either do this from a straight, factual point of view or you could get down to it very deeply and say, "My specialist contribution is really to help that person sort himself out as a person." In the church charity here, you are constantly in the church situation, and you can be the Church-in-practice. It is very obvious that this is so, and you don't have to tell anybody that it is. And people expect so much of the Church. In fact the demands are so much greater. They say, "Why can't you do such-and-such? You're the Church. You should be able to help me solve my problem." . . . If I stay here until I am sixty, I shall think I have done very well.'

Kenneth believed – and it is a common characteristic in people who have had the practical grasp to change careers – that giving did not imply woolly sentimentality. He saw his experience in industry, in so far as it required the taking of hard decisions, as being helpful, even if at the age of fifty he did not want to continue with it.

'Sometimes,' said Kenneth, 'you must say "no" in this job. It is the toughness of that decision which is the necessity for a man in my shoes. Here is a case that springs to mind. We have the role, at one of our homes for old people, of a handyman-gardener who lives on the site and is the *only* man on site. In one particular case, the man was getting married. His wife did not wish to live on site, so they got a house a mile away. He was a perfectly satisfactory employee. But, living a mile away with his wife, he was no longer resident. Now we think this is a particular need in the role. In fact, because he had long service, he had plenty of backers who said we should keep him on in his present job, although he lived a mile away. They said there was a nice, good road to get him back to the home in an emergency. One had to stand out on one's own and say, "We need that man on site. And although we like him and don't want to lose him, he has made this decision not to live on site." You will have to stand up against, not animosity, but harsh criticism, unfairly harsh criticism, when you say, "No. This is what we need in this particular case." Then again, sometimes we have residents in our homes who are really beyond our capacity for caring. We could care for *one* in this situation, but by the time you get two, three, four or even five, you have got to say, "We must part company, otherwise it will break the home." And you have to go to people, perhaps next of kin, and say, "Sorry, we can no longer care for your great-aunt. You have to take her away and do something for her. We can't." . . . I didn't really come across the ruthless side of industry with the oil company, which is the best company in the country . . . Nevertheless, it is big and it is effective and it knows how to do things efficiently and it teaches you how to do this.'

Misjudgement of intimates

In assessing whether someone has a latent giving factor or not, those closest to the person concerned are not necessarily the best judges. They can be so close that all they see is the day-to-day evidence of the past years, as distinct from the promise of the future. It is extremely difficult for anyone to admit that loved ones or acquaintances they have neatly pigeon-holed can have latent powers and possibilities they have not detected.

The case of Robert, the parson who made his way from

accountancy and management consultancy in the first chapter, is an illustration. His mother strongly urged him to stick to business. She told his wife, 'I don't think Robert has got the *caring* for people element which he would need.' His wife (though she backed him up completely when he actually made his move) was inclined to agree with his mother.

Robert's wife recalled to me that she did have this one secret reservation when her husband went on the ordination course:

> 'I used to think to myself, "Well, you know, has he got that understanding and caring for people he would need?" He was very much of a businessman: it was the business that mattered. I did see potentials in him, because he has got an exceedingly good brain, and I knew that he would really work at whatever he did. But I do know that empathy is not just a matter of intellectual equipment. That is the fact I was slightly worried about. His mother was worried, too, when she said she didn't think Robert had got the caring he would need. But that has come. I am thankful to say he has been given that, and I don't think he had it before. Certainly it was there with people he liked, but he had very little patience with people he didn't like. That is something, I think, that he has learnt.'

The interesting point here is that, coming as a complete stranger, he did not strike *me* at all as having a type of personality that I would expect to find in business. Even physically, he seemed miscast for such a role, though evidently the people closest to him – his wife and his mother – had accepted him as perfectly cast. He was tall, spare, and with a fine-featured, rather sensuous face. Not a hustler with a compressed adrenal mouth or cold calculating eyes, or even a bright salesman's manner. His very appearance suggested that his demeanour would be gentle and solicitous; as indeed it was. True, his manner could have changed with his new job, but not his physical appearance. I was left with the conclusion that, with the best will in the world, people who are close to a person can be *too* close to see more than what habit has conditioned them to expect. Robert himself said:

> 'I suppose these "new" factors were there, but because of upbringing and environment, they got put a bit to one side. A thing like this change of vocation gives them an opportunity to come out into the open.'

On reflection, his wife agreed that this might well be so. I, the outsider, never doubted it.

The revealing substitute

It is rare for the giving elements in a human personality to be as completely repressed as they appeared to have been in Robert's case. Usually they express themselves in a tentative way; often in extra-curricular activities to augment a job which has always been unsuitable or which was once suitable but which has now been outgrown.

George, the panel-beater whose path to the probation service was described in Chapter One, took strongly to trade union work when still on the factory floor. Looking back years later, he began to see it as a measure of two things in his character and situation: his dissatisfaction at being on the factory floor and his desire to have a protective role.

> 'If you wanted to get anywhere in my trade, then you had to join the union,' said George. 'I became a very active trade unionist, and a shop steward in the firm I worked for. There was a redundancy of four out of a staff of twenty, and we estimated that if we worked a four-day week until things brightened, we could maintain our labour force. But the management said they would sooner close than work a shorter working week. We all walked out, and that was the first

walk-out we had had in our trade . . . We saw some literature about a particular Commonwealth country, and thought we would go there. You can often get tired of this country; and we were at that time. Plus the fact that I was a bit disillusioned to say the least; not only with the system, but because of the lack of support you got from the members you represented when the chips were down . . . I hadn't learned then that you just have to pick yourself up, dust yourself off and get on with it. I was still very idealistic. My own members of the working class sickened me to a great degree. I went abroad, only to discover when I got there that you can't run away from a work situation or from human beings.'

Back in Britain, he went on with his trade union activities. His memories of them gave me the distinct impression that one of his motives was to protect, as best he could, people whom he saw as his fellow workers; and that he often became paternally irritated with them for not protecting themselves.

Asked whether he was motivated at this stage of his life more by a desire to give than by political or ideological factors, George said: 'A bit of both, really.'

George was surprised when he was nominated to the committee of a prisoners' aid society, which was organising an art exhibition for the work of men in prison. He was even more surprised – as an objective observer of him might not have been – when he was asked by an officer of the society, who was very much *not* of his own political persuasion, 'Why don't you become a probation officer?'

'I said, "Why on earth should I?" remembered George. 'They said, "We think you could be useful. You seem to have the right attitude." '

It was an instance where comparative strangers were better at assessing the psychological implications of his trade union activities than he or the people closest to him were. Had such an objective evaluation been available to him sooner, George would almost certainly have been a more contented and constructive man earlier.

The helpful contrast

It can be helpful if the job currently being followed is in *sharp* contrast to its occupier's notion of giving. The sharper the contrast, the more obvious the message.

There was a vivid contrast in the case of Anthony, a 43-year-old architect who became a disaster mitigation consultant. At the time we met he was studying natural disasters and making recommendations on how the results, in terms of damage and death, could be minimised. He was attached to a university, where his salary was less than it would have been had he stayed in straight architecture.

> 'I think there was a certain social conscience that made me leave architecture,' said Anthony. 'Perhaps not a very large thing. But the potential for making money was there in architecture. I had been doing it for fifteen years, and academic's salaries are sticky. I certainly didn't make the change for the money. I come from a very ordinary middle-class suburban family. My father worked in a bank, and he reads the *Daily Telegraph*. But I think the image sometimes applied to architecture is unfortunate. Glossy expensive buildings in cities, which may or may not be successful – bearing in mind what happened with tower blocks. Rich people. So, to people who aren't really attuned to what architecture is, it means the standards of coffee-table books. People's image of architecture is rich and highly decorative, whereas really architecture's function is in solving problems in a physical way, through the provision of a building. Many of these problems are nothing to do with the glossy – they are the provision of schools,

hospitals and universities to very tight cost limits and time schedules . . . Architecture, to me, is therefore a humanitarian pursuit. If there is a gap between that and disasters in the Third World, it is not a very great one.'

But the gap Anthony contemplated in his own professional life was rather larger than that. He was working on an expensive tunnel project overseas.

> 'It was the year of the big cyclone in Bangladesh. I wondered whether things were going as well as they should from the point of view of relief. I was certainly beginning to feel I wanted to do something else, especially when I worked in expensive buildings among poor people. I was becoming interested in doing other things than creating striking buildings.'

Benevolent impulses and professional thoughts fused into one line of reasoning: that he could best help by concentrating not on disaster relief *after* the event, but in pre-planning to avoid the worst results. He combined a research job in the developing centre of his university with a freelance practice as a disaster mitigation consultant, working from an attic office in his terraced stone cottage.

All this was provoked by his awareness that there was a *clear* gap between what he was doing previously and the living conditions of the people among whom he did it. The more unambiguous the discrepancy, the more the likelihood of prompt action.

The dangers of frittering

Finally, the impulse towards giving faces a worse enemy than selfishness (which is more readily recognisable): a failure to channel a general generous impulse into a specific beneficial activity.

Elizabeth joined a religious order when she was eighteen. She went to a teacher training college at the request of her Order while at the same time continuing her religious training. She finished both sets of training and, at the age of 24, taught in an aided Catholic school. At the time of our interview, she had temporarily left behind her nun's habit to run a local Association of Youth.

She is a lively person with sharp, light grey eyes. I would say her businesslike manner was probably acquired rather than innate.

'I have always been afraid of getting into a rut,' said Elizabeth. She has had many changes of job and acknowledged that it was having the discipline of a religious order that had enabled her to cope without frittering herself away.

> 'It is always difficult, looking back, to analyse why, at such an early age, I had determined on a religious life. But I always felt a kind of philanthropic bent in me. It sounds terribly old-fashioned now, but I think that is at the root of it. I am sure that one of the motives in joining the religious life was that I was free to help other people. I hadn't sufficient understanding, at that time, of the community or of deep spirituality. I always wanted to help everybody everywhere. To me, the religious life was a way of channelling my helping. Someone would help me choose a particular angle rather than let me be all over the place, as I had been before I became religious.'

A concrete goal, as well as a general impulse to help, is necessary to all those who aspire to change their lives in the direction of more generous activities. If an institutional basis for this discipline cannot be found, it must be found in the human individual himself.

CHAPTER FOUR: BACK TO SCHOOL

Most people who change their occupations substantially when past the first blush of youth have to adapt to intensive study at an unusual age. This will either be undertaken academically, before the new job is started, or at a practical level while actually doing the job. How frightening do people, no longer young, find this process? And is the fear justified?

In some cases a late start can have advantages. Alison went to public school and then on to a college to learn how to be a librarian. She became a librarian in a Commonwealth country at first 'because they were a great deal more outgoing in what they did – they had children's books weeks and got children to the library to listen to stories, whereas in England we tended to be very passive. The books were just there for the children to borrow. Over there, we actually went out and encouraged children to use the library.'

Though Alison gave me the 'standard answer' when I asked her why she had become a librarian in the first place – 'One likes books more than one likes people' – it was perhaps forseeable, from her preference for the overseas system, that she would gravitate towards a job where people mattered relatively more and books less.

She joined a provincial paper as librarian, worked for a stockbroker, went abroad again for two years, worked in the technical library of a tobacco firm, and then was with a training board for six years, setting up its library and involving herself in personnel training.

It was at this point, when she was nearly 31, that she went 'back to school'.

> 'This was the first time, I think, that I found a subject matter which really interested me more than the technique of librarianship. Obviously some people are more suited to working in technical fields and previously I had been quite happy to apply the techniques of librarianship to that. But when I went to the training board, I found that I was more interested in the actual subject matter – the training of people – and I started going to evening classes to study the subject matter.'

This was before she thought of a basic change of direction in her employment.

> 'I just wanted to increase my background knowledge. There were evening classes in personnel management, mostly at a technical college. I was coming up to 31 when I started studying at the evening classes. I put in six hours a week at the college and in addition one had to set aside about three or four hours of one's own time. But I didn't find any problems taking it at that age, compared with what I would have done had I taken it when I left school. It was interesting and I was interested in it. I think I was actually helped by the fact that, while I was doing theory during the course, I was involved with people who were directly engaged in personnel management, even though I was not practising the practical side of it myself. It all dovetailed nicely. If I learned about the theories of motivation as part of my college course, it was extremely useful when people wanted books for information on these subjects from my library. The whole thing integrated. It was quite hard work, but I didn't find it difficult, because my interest was captured. I think

personnel management is a subject that is *better* studied later on than, say, at eighteen or nineteen. It is one of those subjects where the more experience you have got yourself, and the more understanding you have of people, the more sense it makes to you in studying it.'

A fusing of the techniques of one's present job with the new subject being studied is obviously an ideal situation. The one enhances the interest of the other, and feeds it with new energy. Such a course, as in the case of Alison, may well appear easy. But even if the present job is so boring that further academic studies connected with it merely add to the frustration, the long-term results can still be useful in a newer and more interesting job.

Alison went into a local authority to set up its information systems, only to find that the authority was unprepared to allow her to put her suggestions into practice. Before she discovered this, she was already, at 38, studying for an MA in public administration, having started when she was 36. This time she found it heavy going.

'It was incredibly difficult, because it was such a boring subject,' she said, 'and I wasn't anything like as committed to it. It was a taught MA. Most MAs are done by thesis or research work, but there are a few that are taught in the same way as an undergraduate who gets a BA is taught. I therefore had to attend a polytechnic one day a week for six terms. That was almost a waste of time, because we got little help from the tutors. Most of the sessions I found either extremely boring or extremely difficult to understand. Really, when it came down to it, it was the work one did on one's own that counted; and this was very much harder than the evening classes in personnel management had been. I wasn't as committed, and it was a totally different subject. So I had a lot of catching up to do on the background information, whereas most of my fellow students were already lecturing in public administration for Ordinary National or Higher National Certificates, and they had the basic grounding. I didn't have any of this. It was a long, hard grind. I think I found the subject boring because I found my particular job boring. I never really got into local government, so to speak. I am quite prepared to admit that a large proportion of it was probably my fault.'

However, the apparently useless study was of indirect use to her when she made a major change of job at the age of 38. She took a job with a body concerned with education for business.

> 'I think the fact that, when I was in local government, I had embarked on an MA in public administration, counted in my favour when I applied for the new job, though the actual nature of the subject had no direct connection with them at all,' said Alison. 'I think they were perhaps impressed with the fact that I was doing this in my spare time. Certainly, if I got it, the possession of an MA would be very helpful in the educational field, and it is the possession of it, rather than the subject matter, which is important.'

Her new job was an example of how, in some cases of 'going back to school', the new job itself *is* the school. This can be as nerve-wracking, but ultimately rewarding, as academic training.

It is not unusual for such a way of 'going back to school' to be accompanied by feelings of demoralisation, of being less of a person. Did this apply to Alison?

> 'The first few months, I think I was more confused than anything. I was having to come to terms with a completely new environment and new job. Each particular field or profession definitely has its own jargon, and education is by no means an exception to this. There was also a different way of operating,

because further education is definitely a distinct field of it own. The first three months, I really felt all at sea. I was frantically trying to catch up and establish a new framework for myself. This, coming when I was 38, did, to a certain extent, affect my confidence in myself. I had been used to being in a situation where I was known as somebody who was doing a good job; I was looked up to and respected. In a sense I had more or less come to take that for granted, to count on it. The change certainly did affect my confidence.'

She followed one inviolate rule: nothing must show on the surface. However, she was aware of it within herself. The symptoms were characteristic. At staff meetings she tended not to say very much. This was partly because she did not want to risk exposing her ignorance and partly because she did not want to be identified with judgements too quickly, before she had been able to take in the whole situation.

In dealing with this lack of confidence, her relatively mature years were a distinct help, not a hindrance.

'I don't think that, except for very close acquaintances, anyone would have been overly aware of my lack of confidence,' she said. 'That is one of the benefits of age, that you can *conceal things more* than when you are sixteen, seventeen or eighteen. I certainly had to bring that into play when I first started giving talks at conferences or meetings. Because of being short-staffed, we couldn't afford to go and visit individual colleges. We accepted invitations to speak as part of a conference, or ran a one-day conference, or addressed a meeting where several colleges came together. So you tend to have anything from twenty to a hundred people in the room together. Certainly the first few times I talked to them, I had to bring all my deceptive arts, or whatever you like to call them, into play to make sure that I wasn't appearing as nervous as I was inside.

'Also, I was very conscious that I had never worked in a college and never taught, and certainly didn't know the ins-and-outs of the way college courses were administered. I knew quite well that a lot of the questions I would get in the question-and-answer sessions would be related to this and I was very aware that revealing my ignorance at that stage could destroy my credibility. It was a case of having to think very quickly and give answers that would indicate that I was aware of their problems, but not give away the fact that it was the first time, in some cases, that I had even *heard* of such problems . . .

'I certainly wouldn't rule out another complete change at some time in the future. I would certainly view it with a very open mind, shall we say. I think that if you have changed your direction once it is a lot easier to do it another time, because you have the confidence of knowing you have done it once. The feelings of insecurity would not be new to you and you'd hope they would not last for as long as before. In my case, they lasted perhaps three or four months. Without being able to put a finger on it precisely, there came a time when I realised that, without knowing as much as all my colleagues, I certainly knew enough. I had built myself, if you like, a new framework: I knew where I was. There were still a lot of gaps in my knowledge but I knew where they were. I knew my strengths in such-and-such an area and my weaknesses too. Suddenly I was aware that I was on top of the job rather than struggling in the deep end.'

From hand to brain

For Alison, the move was from one cerebral job to

another, a transference of 'brainwork'. A move to a cerebral job from one with a manual content may entail a more humiliating, and longer, period of feeling oneself back in school, with one's knees figuratively scraping against the bottom of the desk.

George, the panel-beater who became a probation officer, and whose impulses towards more giving were dealt with in the last chapter, found the theoretical part of the course he had to take 'very threatening'. It was one of the most extreme instances of unease in all the job-changers I spoke to: an authoritarian personality suddenly turned into a raw beginner though he was 'the Daddy of the course'. George was candid on the subject of his fears about his own intellect.

> 'Here I was, having spent nineteen years in factory work. What office work I had done had been voluntarily for my trade union. I hadn't written any essays or reports or anything of that kind, so my knowledge of English was very small. I had got a first and second year technical English certificate when I had been at night school, and that was all. So I had fears.'

They were not foreseen at the very start of his changeover process.

> 'In those days,' he recalled, 'you applied to the Home Office and then you went for an hour's interview with a Home Office inspector. Then they assessed whether or not it was worth you taking the next step. About two months after that, I went for a whole day to the Home Office. They gave me an intelligence test and I was interviewed by a committee of three. I discussed my philosophy and told them about my trade union activities. They decided I should be accepted. I then began my actual training course which, as far as I was concerned, was very easy. I

was given a case load of about ten or twelve people and allowed to interview my clients. It all seemed very easy to me. I did dabble in some reports on clients; perhaps two or three. By then, three months later, I went for the theoretical course. That lasted three months. I found that very threatening.'

The subjects he studied were human growth and development, probation practice, law and case work. They involved a greater degree of academic thinking than he had been used to. But the main difficulty was feeling confident among his colleagues on the same course. 'It was a very intense time for me,' said George.

One can easily see why. He was in his forties. It was a course for mature students; but the youngest was only 27, a fact which emphasised his own age.

> 'Then I found that people from university were there,' said George. 'This was a course which then had to be followed whether you had a degree or not: it was an orientation course. The most threatening thing was that it was something completely out of my ken, although I had spent two weeks in a college summer school. I went for one week and then won a scholarship to go there the following year, so I had a little insight, in a small way, into what university life could be like. . . But what I now found was that by this time I desperately *wanted* to become a probation officer and I was afraid of not achieving it. It was the reverse of the previous situation, when I had not cared. This time I really did care. It became quite frightening to me when I thought I wouldn't make the grade.'

He found comforting points of reference at this time, in the same way that many people do in his position: through his children. His son was eighteen and engaged in his A levels, and his daughter was sixteen and working on her O levels. Reversing the usual role, *they* gave support to *him* in his studies. He went to them, and they gave him advice.

He failed the casework part of his examination, largely because of his tension.

> 'It affected my morale pretty badly, because I remembered the trade union adage that before you can become a good trade unionist you must learn your trade. And here was I, at that time in my life, in a trade at which I felt I was a baby. And I felt very threatened. For the first eighteen months to two years I just worked hard at everything I was given. Like all willing horses, I got exploited. It came to a caseload of 59. I don't think any of us had much time then. That was average at that time, 59 juveniles. It went up to 74 in the next 3 or 4 years. I did 84 reports in my first six months. I remember the morning when I was interviewed at the end of my course – and I fluffed the casework exam and had to re-sit it. I was a bit late, and I walked into the room where there were lots of cups and saucers for cups of tea. I poured the tea and picked the cup up, and it was really shaking. I remember someone saying to me, "Is it as bad as that, George?" And I said, "Yes, it is." That was before I sat the exam. It was not surprising that I failed; I just went numb.'

In this state, he made a classic error: he was over-eager. He *wanted* to seem keen. To his examiners – as he did not realise until afterwards – he seemed merely unrealistic. The circumstances add up to a general warning against appearing too glib in a new occupation.

The candidates had to consider the problem of what they would hope to achieve at first interview with a little girl who was having problems at home.

'I put *all* my hopes down,' said George. 'I realised

very soon afterwards that it was foolish, because the hopes I had given were what you would hope to achieve in a long time, not at first interview. I wrote down, with great enthusiasm, that I would hope to make a friendship with her, to be able to win her confidence, to be able to influence her to obey her parents, and all this sort of thing. Whereas in reality, all you could hope to achieve on a first interview would be to get perhaps even the basis of some beginning to a relationship; which would enable you, perhaps, in months or years, to develop all the hopes I had written down. That was what they were looking for: was I sensitive enough to be able to realise that whatever happened would take such a long time? When I sat the exam again, I took a realistic view. What happened on the previous occasion was really because I was knotted up about sitting an exam.'

George took his children's advice on the law side of the examinations, and passed. He asked them, 'How am I going to get through?' They said, 'Write down what you think you have got to learn and, before you go to sleep each night, read it through.' He did it for three weeks each night. It worked.

But his inhibitions about the use of English, and about court procedure, stayed with him for a long time. 'I suspect that my tutor had said that I lacked experience in written work; and it seems to me that once something like that gets in your dossier, it haunts you,' said George.

After the theoretical course, he and five others were sent to a training unit. They went out to courts, then came back to have case discussions and make reports. His reports were greatly cut about at first; he estimated it took him two to three years to feel at home when using words. The period was possibly lengthened because of his own inhibitions.

'My reports were always inspected and vetted, with the idea that you achieve a certain standard fairly quickly. But when you are writing reports and you know you will submit them to someone who is going to carve them up, it becomes a very sensitive matter. Psychologically, then, it becomes almost a terror. It used to worry me that a fully grown man could be subjected to this sort of feeling.'

He overcome it, basically, because he eventually realised that his own industrial background could be an active advantage (not merely a grammatical embarrassment) in his new job. A boy came before a juvenile court. George had to prepare a psychiatric report, his first. He submitted his report direct to the psychiatrist of the Home Office without anyone else seeing it. The psychiatrist opened *his* report on the boy with the observation, 'I have read an excellent background report by Mr George —— on this boy.'

'That made up for all the psychological and emotional sufferings that I had felt in going back to school, as it were,' said George. 'After that, I thought – and still do – that provided reports are logical and written in English, they are useful. We all have various prejudices about writing reports and not everyone agrees about what makes a good report. I came from a working class background, as you may imagine from my elementary schooling. I had been kept away from school a long time, and I hadn't always talked as freely as I do now because I had a country accent. I will only say that I do have some understanding of the people I am often dealing with. I have trotted to the pawnshop – it was a regular trip as a child. I understand that the five to seven per cent we deal with, as professional social workers, will be in the lower income group. Having come from that sort of background myself, I do understand their financial problems to a degree. Also, when it comes to work, well, my factory work was probably the best you can get; but I had worked for a time on the mass production line of a car firm and I understand the utter boredom that exists in many of the modern unskilled jobs that are available. I understand the deadly monotony. I also have been able to make a good list of employers who would give people jobs. That went by the board with the extreme unemployment situation of the mid-1970s, but when I first came here, I went round and saw the personnel managers or anyone necessary. I would often find work for the clients of other officers.'

I asked George if the experience of feeling humiliatingly threatened as an adult man had made him stronger. He thought it had.

'Yes, in this respect,' he said. 'In a way – and I say this with all humility – in the first two or three years I came into this job I undervalued myself, because I felt inferior. . . No, I *considered* myself inferior to the other people. And then it suddenly dawned upon me that other people were beginning to ask *my* opinion about cases.'

The initial humiliation he suffered benefited him in a further way. Where younger probation officers coming into the profession from an academic background tended, in his opinion, to look for very specific 'success' and were cast down when their clients did not immediately oblige, his weathered personality was more able to accept that success in his job usually existed only in terms of *degrees*, not absolutes.

'I accept the fact,' he said, 'that to *look* for success can only be frustrating. You get measures of success and you get successful clients, where they do make it. But to expect success of a high level can only end in disappointment and frustration. If it does work, it is great. But I am very interested in how you measure terms of success. How is success measured in the habitual criminal, the man who has to return to prison all his life?'

George acquired a more robust attitude to academic forms of learning.

'I think it made a difference, leaving it until late, in that I had a greater life experience. Although there is much you can learn from written knowledge and written books, there are two educations you get in this life. One you get from others and one you give yourself. And I think the one you give yourself is just as important, if not more so, than the one you get from other people. I think it is an active benefit that I waited until I was in my forties before training as a probation officer. I think you need a great deal of maturity to deal with clients. But now they don't have the selection procedure I went through. They go to a polytechnic or a college or a university because of their academic ability; and because they come out at the end of two or three years doesn't necessarily mean that they are the best people to be social workers or probation officers.'

George said that he would now not hesitate to study for a degree if he felt it necessary. One of the questions on his course was, 'The middle-aged social worker says, "I am the only one sitting here without a degree." What is your immediate reaction?'

'My reaction,' said George, 'is that it is never too late. If I felt strongly that I wanted a degree, then I would go to the Open University. It may well be that people would say I ought to do that, but I don't feel the need. I don't feel the lack as much as I did when I first came into the job. I find the psychiatrists are just as anxious to know my opinion as I am to know theirs.'

In short, George's temporary plunge in confidence has resulted, in the longer-term, in far greater personal resilience.

Mannerism magnification

The older person moving among younger people in his studies may encounter taxing and humiliating social difficulties as well as academic ones. If faced squarely, the final product can be positive rather than negative.

Gerald, a former theatre worker who became a security man abroad, returned to this country to run a hostel for ex-prisoners, and then realised it might not be compatible with marrying a younger and better educated woman. There followed the major academic change in his life. In discussing his possible future among his wife-to-be's friends (who, he admitted, had wider intellectual horizons than himself at that time), the possibility of his becoming a probation officer was mentioned.

> 'Initially,' said Gerald, 'I had no confidence in myself or my abilities to do anything of any value or to bring in enough money to keep us. I had no qualifications. It was something that my wife said that encouraged me, and of course meeting her friends. I had seen probation officers and was highly critical of them. I thought I could do a better job, in a thoughtful way. Eventually I was persuaded to apply, so I applied first of all to the Home Office. There were four courses which were recognised by the Probation Service and I applied for one of them. Hundreds had applied and I didn't see any reason why I should be chosen. But I was lucky. I think what may have commended me was my age and the fact that I had spent two and a half years in a hostel for ex-prisoners. I think the youngest person on the course was about 23 and I, at 49, was the second oldest. I found the theoretical side of the course

difficult, but not humiliating. The only humiliating moments were more *social*, nothing to do with the course itself. They were purely of my own making and, in retrospect, laughable.'

It was easy to see, when we met, that Gerald could have struck social difficulties. He was a man with a quiet manner that somehow managed to be larger than life. Without in any way being obvious or loud, his demeanour did vaguely suggest that he had indeed spent many years of his life in the theatre. His manner was polite and pleasant but, even when he was whispering, one detected elements of the stage whisper, audible in the gallery. This generously large manner, amiable among contemporaries could – and sometimes did – strike people who were younger as being patronising.

'I had a young tutor, a girl of about 26,' said Gerald with a good-natured smile. 'In tutorials, there were six or seven of us. Well, I don't care who it is, I always call women I know "Love". And in tutorial this young lady really put me down. She was very much Women's Lib, and she decided I was putting *her* down. I can easily see how she thought that, though of course it wasn't true. Perhaps I *was* doing the 49-year-old thing. Perhaps I was a bit nervous of her qualifications. Maybe, without knowing it, I *was* putting her down. But I couldn't change it. It was an expression I used, whether it was to a woman prison governor or anyone else; just as when I see an elderly gentleman and, no matter whether he is on Skid Row or not, provided he is older than me, I call him "Sir". I say, "Well, sir, now what can I do for you?" It is just a thing I got from home and from the theatre. But this young lady tutor couldn't understand that.

'At the end of the course she did say to me, when I brought it up, "Gerry,the day you *stop* calling me 'Love', I shall think there is something wrong." But

> at the time she put me down for it, it really set me aback. It is the little things like that which can be humiliating, when you speak from what you think is your experience, and you are slapped down by a person much younger, and you can see how they're absolutely right.'

There were bad moments, too, in the tea-group encounters when discussion entailed a great deal of soul-baring. It is just the sort of situation in which an older person, speaking when his guard is relaxed, can cause, and suffer, misunderstandings. Gerald, half knowing this, nevertheless decided to stick to the principle he had formed early and 'have a bash'.

> 'And of course I *did* have a bash, and of course some of my ideas were really shot down,' he said. 'But of course, you could sometimes see where your long experience of living was of value to your colleagues. You want to give, but in other people's eyes it can sometimes seem an affectation. You have to manage the situation as best you can with your own individual personality. If they see you are genuine, that is OK. When I say anything, I don't preach, it is a gut feeling, and that is OK. But if at any time the younger people – who of course are feeling threatened *themselves* in various academic ways – think it is an affectation, they will sit on it. So you suddenly find that they sit on something which is a gut feeling in you and *not* an affectation, and then it hurts. You are emotionally affronted in a way you weren't prepared for.'

It is quite common for complicated and taxing social dealings to result in poor academic results. Equally it is common for academic results to improve once the social atmosphere has improved. It was so in Gerald's case.

Gerald was over-conscious, at first, that the people he

was mixing with were academically, and perhaps intellectually, his superiors. He had been used to assimilating only from experience. He had done nothing by way of formal study in all his adult life.

> 'From a very early age, my bookshelves, wherever I was, were filled with non-fiction. Teach yourself this, teach yourself that. I suppose I was looking for an education I had lost. But of course it was a grasshopper learning, in the sense that I didn't settle on any one thing. So it became very much of a challenge. One was very conscious – in fact, over-conscious – that the people you were mixing with were intellectually your superiors, though they were often younger. It was my wife who taught me not to feel like that. I would go to a party with her friends and say, "Well, I held my end up there." And she would say, "Of course you did. Why shouldn't you?" I had an academic inferiority complex, and probably still have. That meant that for the first eight or nine months of the course, I hardly opened my mouth. It's true. I think I re-established my self-respect with the help of my colleagues, in the end. It was the change in their attitude to me that gave me confidence in myself. It was because people would come and talk to me and discuss things with me. And of course it was from the results of the course itself, because you get continuous assessment.'

One of the penalties of a repressed social life, when studying with people younger than oneself, is that there is a tendency to 'splurge' in examination papers when the technique should be more spare and exact. Gerald made this mistake.

> 'In essay writing,' he remembered, 'I got good results, but not at the beginning. The first essay I put in carried a pass mark of forty. My first psychology

essay copped forty. I was most offended. I had started at six at night and finished at about four in the morning. But, of course, after I had got the essay back, I looked at it and thought, "I haven't answered the question. I have done a lot of splurge, a great splurge which got me forty marks, but it is nothing to do with the question." My next three essays all got seventy. That was fine. My self-esteem was reinforced. The rest were up to that sort of mark. That had a marvellous way of encouraging me and making me feel more confident in myself.'

The natural actor in him at first complicated not only his social relationships but also his academic results. His second year tutor was a rather solemn man.

'A very good man and I was very lucky to have him. But he didn't appreciate my essays at all. It was not my academic grasp, it was my manner. I got good enough marks, between sixty and seventy, and that was fine. But my inclination was to be very ironic, to look for the humorous side. When I could put a bit of humour into it, great! In my best essay, I got a mark of about eighty for law. It was marked by a man who had a wonderful sense of humour. It was academically satisfactory, but it had these elements of irony and humour. The main criticism was, "This is journalism, not academic." '

The serious crime of 'journalism' told against him at first; but on reflection he decided to stick to this approach when writing out his reports as a probation officer. He thought it was more useful if he reported not only the facts, but also presented to his seniors his thoughts on what was happening. 'Fortunately my immediate senior has a sense of humour.'

The fact remains that to pass examinations, it is necessary to provide what examiners want *in the way they want it*, keeping one's adult mannerisms in reserve. The danger is that, threatened, such mannerisms may become over-assertive, and prejudice both academic work and social relations with younger fellow-students.

The student life that never was

The man or woman who becomes a student at a later age than average may be handicapped by the sad thought that he has missed for ever the easy, unforced informal student life that would have been granted him naturally had he been younger. He may conjure up visions of an idyllic time that he has missed. It may be self-deceit. (Is youthful student life really so free of strains? Twenty-year-old students would have their own view on that.) It is certainly a fruitlessly self-indulgent line of thought.

However, it remains common and excusable. Mervyn, who switched from being an insurance auditor to studying to be a parson at the age of 49, was a victim to some extent. This was when he took an ordination course designed to train men for the Ministry while they are simultaneously doing their accustomed daily work.

When I asked Mervyn what his feelings had been when he was encountering his working strains during the day and coping with his studies in the evenings or weekends, he said at once, 'I was always on a wave of enthusiasm.' Then he thought further and added.

> 'Occasionally I used to feel rather downcast and aware of my own inadequacies. The ordination course was a very good course. But if you compare it with going to a theological college, where you probably study and attend a few lectures in the morning, have a bit of tennis in the afternoon and read in the evening in a relaxed atmosphere . . . You would have time to think there, time to read all around a subject, but we were under pressure the whole time. One sometimes felt, on being given a list of six books to read for one particular lecture, that

> it was a total impossibility. And one had to get hold of as many books as one could. From this point of view, one felt inadequacy.'

The central fact is that, in constructing any system of study for late entrants, those responsible know that unless the student is prepared and able to absorb such hard shocks (which need not be administered to those who do their studies at the more normal age) he is unlikely to change his own life in middle age or near middle age. A high fence to climb is often provided at the first part of the academic combat course.

It was so in the ordination course faced by Mervyn. There was no invitation to the Elysian fields popularly supposed to be occupied by students. Mervyn said of the man who conducted the first interview with him:

> 'He gave me one of the most dusty interviews I have ever had in my life. I have come across crusty Brigadiers and all sorts of people, but this man had a method of interrogation which stripped one down utterly. In the end I felt like saying, "I'm sorry I asked." He did this by being very critical of what one had done. One of the questions was this: if I had felt so strongly about the Church, why hadn't I done something about it earlier? I told him I had had this burning desire all the time but hadn't felt the way was clear to act on it, for family reasons. Later I got a letter saying he was recommending me for a place. But that was his method of interrogation. A fair one? I don't really think it brings out the best in people. I think it may bring out the best in *some* people, but if they are shy and retiring it doesn't work. But I suppose it is fair to say that you need to be tough if you are going to change your way of life. I remember a bright young friend of mine joining a religious community. He was immediately put in a field of mangel-wurzels, and had to spend day after day picking them. The idea was to break his spirit for

him, so that after a few days he would say, "I'm not staying here." That was their policy, I suppose.'

Mervyn had to admit candidly to himself that he would have found the form of study that was expected of him much easier at 19 than at 49. He faced the fact head-on and *attacked* it, unlike some in a similar position who comfort themselves by thinking of the advantages they have over young people. (Either method is valid if it works in practice.)

'At the age of 49, after being in commercial life, one was not quite so used to academic study, and could not take to it as well as one could just after leaving school. One hadn't the resilience. One had the keenness, yes, but not the resilience of youth in studying. I used to come home, have my dinner, go into the other room and shut the door. I would have books around and often *I* would be around until two o'clock in the morning. I would not retire until I had finished. I don't think these are the ideal conditions for working, but I did get a certain kick out of them. When I went to bed I was completely tired out, but I had the satisfaction of having accomplished what I had set out to do. I can get away with five or six hours' sleep.'

Mervyn said he thought that his most testing time as a student might have been easier if his daily job had been something he frankly disliked, and in which he didn't *need* therefore to be a respectable success.

'I was promoted to chief clerk in the firm. I had a very good team in the department. I like to think I was successful in having a happy and efficient team. Some people are ruthless in demanding efficiency, but I always thought the way I worked was to have a happy team. I was lucky, I suppose, that I had very good men under me, but I then delegated to them. Some people suggested I should delegate everything after I started the ordination course, but that wasn't my idea at all. As a keen churchman I never liked to think I was falling down on the job. On top of that, on the course we had to pass two exams a year. If we didn't pass we felt the Sword of Damocles hanging over us, as we were never quite sure whether we would be out in three and a half years, or what would happen.'

Mervyn was among those job-changers I talked to who most emphasised the disadvantages of studying late in life, and the sadness of missing the time of study in one's youth. I asked him what advice he would give to others after his own experience.

'I would say, if I had my time over again and could profit from my experience, I would go into the Church early on. Whilst people are kind enough to say, "Ah, but you bring all the experience of the commercial world" and so on, I have found that in the Church one has missed out on so much experience as a priest. Indeed, one has missed out so much experience on this side of the fence, as it were, that I don't know how it balances out. People often say they can talk to me more than to someone a little more academic. Well, I don't know how that evens out.

'When you come to discuss with your fellow clergy questions which are academic, you find they have been through university and perhaps are younger – a generation away – and they switch about intellectually and have a resilience which possibly I don't have. Most modern youth, like my own sons, have a personal assurance about themselves that I have never really felt. So many young people have opportunity. They have two or three A levels. They get grants – not easily, but they are able to scrape by on them. They take this as a right rather than a privilege. I possibly envy them in that respect, but I think it is a good thing that they feel like that and a good thing that they should have that assurance.'

Those who see greater merit in Mervyn and his way of becoming a parson than he is able to see for himself, might argue that he was merely rationalising a rather self-doubting nature; and that self-assurance has an ultimate value only when it is justified by actual merit. They might also think that his sense of being cut off from youthful student pleasures was an expression of his temperament rather than of the objective facts. One way or the other, his feelings are shared by many who change their jobs later in life, but are not necessarily crippling. Mervyn's own transition is proof of that.

The new words barrier

Educational methods have changed greatly in the past twenty years; so have their vocabularies. It is a fact which has created more difficulties for those going 'back to school' today than would have been created for people taking the same step a generation ago.

Ben, the draughtsman who became a primary school teacher, was 43 when he was accepted by a teacher training college.

> 'I found it slightly different and difficult at first because of the language, which I found had altered since I left school. They were using lots of big words, of which I did not know the meaning. They explained and I said, "There are two ordinary words that would do for that one particular word." So I had to translate everything. The children who had just come from school, the eighteen-year-olds, seemed to have been brought up in this way of thinking and talking. I didn't even know what the word "bibliography" meant. They would churn this word out, but it took me some time to find out what it

meant, as I had never come across it before. When you look back at books, you find they only started using bibliographies, described as such, about twenty or thirty years ago. Previously to that, they had given references but never called it a bibliography. Yes, vocabulary was the most difficult part of it. When I wrote my essays I had to refer a lot to dictionaries. In psychology and sociology I had psychological and sociological dictionaries which actually gave the specific words. To put it another way, I found that words had different meanings in these fields. I had been using a word for years, but in psychology or sociology it had a different meaning.

All the people on the course with Ben were mature students, but their ages varied fairly widely. Not only did Ben find the younger men and women more familiar with the vocabulary, which was faintly humiliating, but they were also physically fitter.

> 'We older ones tried to act the same as they did in most things,' said Ben. 'A lot of the course was to do with physical education. We took part in every physical education lesson, and did everything they did, though sometimes we paid for it. If you do perhaps a dozen forward rolls you soon know you have a backbone. The younger ones most probably didn't experience what we did, but we wouldn't give up. I know for a fact that when we went in, we found it a wee bit of a struggle to adapt to a new way of life, to a new way of thinking, to being instructed again, and the eighteen-year-olds didn't.'

But Ben found it to be a rather different story as the long gruelling course progressed. The balance of advantage then turned *towards* the older students.

'Our age carried us through,' he said. 'At the end of three years, we felt it was easy. But the eighteen-year-olds were then finding it difficult. A lot of girls, and some of the boys, were on tranquillizers, which we couldn't see the point of. Our maturity wouldn't let us rely on them: we were more self-starters and steadier-goers. It seemed that the maturer students were more stable than the youngsters were. Our age gave us the ability to cope with difficulties and stress.'

When the students on this course went out on teaching practices each year, it was in fact one of the most unnerving ways of 'going back to school' themselves; they were very much under critical observation and were unused to addressing very young people. It was harder in this respect, claimed Ben, for the older students at the course than for the younger ones.

'The last thing I could remember about schooling was being lectured *to* in the fifth year,' he said. 'That wasn't teaching, it wasn't *showing* people. It is difficult to explain the difference, but lecturing is just sort of *telling* people what to do and where to look for the necessary information. Teaching is *showing* people the way through, showing them how to find out things from experiment or by play. A lot of it is play and exploration in junior school teaching. You have to build up very slowly. Each step has to be taken separately, without assuming that they know anything. The eighteen-year-olds at college could always relate mentally to their siblings, because most of them had brothers and sisters of ten and eleven years old. The age difference between me, forty-five-odd, and the ten-year-olds was so wide. I only felt I was beating this particular difficulty on my third teaching practice.'

During his probationary year as a teacher, Ben did not

encounter the same difficulties as on the teacher-training course. He estimated that he might well (having had thoroughly and consciously to learn the techniques of teaching young children) have encountered fewer problems at this stage than people who had started teacher-training at an earlier age would have done.

'I worked,' said Ben, 'and I still do, *alongside* them, in an open-plan school. Two classes side by side. The deputy head appreciated my experience outside and when it came to a lesson on, say, plastics, I was able to give a fairly good demonstration, having learned the subject at the firm I once worked for. When it came to science or technical drawing, when we started doing compass work and that sort of thing, my outside experience was valuable. On one occasion when I was teaching my class (of course with open-plan you can see exactly what the other class is doing), the deputy headmaster said, "I will do the next lesson with your class and will you do the next lesson with mine?" He appreciated my experience and it worked out extremely well. It still works out well. I am still there.

'My most serious doubts about the whole process were after two years at the teacher-training college. I began to wonder whether I would pass out at the end of the third year. It worried me a wee bit to think I had gone on for two years, but would I finally succeed in becoming a teacher? It was continuous assessment, there were no exams on this course, but I would begin to worry about essays that I had to write. However, when I got ABs, or B-pluses, I got a real boost. I felt, "I am on top of this, I have no need to worry." And I enjoyed the last teaching practice, as opposed to the previous two, which were a bit of a bind. What difficulties there were, at the teacher training college and later, soon lessened. I think my maturity actually helped me there.'

Age makes practice easier

Older students can set against their initial humiliations the thought that when they come to apply their learning in practice, they will probably find it easier than a younger person who has known academic life and nothing else.

Andrea, 34 at the time of our interview, was just off to work as an occupational therapist abroad. It was part of her plan to gain varied experience to make up for her late start in the profession. She had worked in telecommunications inside and outside the Forces. Faced with redundancy in a civilian job, she was worried because she had no A levels, but was referred to a women's college which allowed her to take a year's course (usually for students preparing to go to university) without A levels.

> 'I was about 28 or 29 when I went,' said Andrea. 'Most of them would be around 30, give or take a few years, but there was a handful of people over the 45 mark. I had a double struggle, studying at 29. I am not an academic by any means, but having been in the Services in telecommunications I was taught a lot of technical stuff because you go on course after course. You just learn it by rote. You learn everything in an abbreviated form, and you just absorb it like blotting paper. I was brainwashed into learning that way. To get to the college was the most fantastic thing that ever happened to me, because you had to sit down and analyse everything, exactly as one would do if one were at university. It was designed more as a foundation course to a university course than anything else. If only I had done that when I left the Forces! I felt I had wasted seven years, and had a compulsion to make up for that loss. I was a student for four years: at the college and at a school of occupational therapy. I struggled with the occupational therapy course, the academic bit, the anatomy and physiology – I had never done any science subjects before. I had done geography,

history, commerce, economics, all those things instead, so I was struggling. But in the end I suppose I caught up, because the exam results proved that I had quite a lot of credits towards the end.'

Why did she think this had happened after a difficult start?

'I suppose one does take a more mature view than one would have done had one been younger. In a way, you can *see the wood for the trees*, whereas the youngsters can't. Most of the girls at the occupational therapy college were straight from school. Whilst they were whizzing through the academic bit, they reached a stumbling block when they were faced with patients and had no idea what to do with them, how to handle them, how to work out realistic treatment programmes for them, and so on. They just hadn't had the experience of dealing with people. So it worked out in the end.'

The discipline benefit

There can be a further advantage, this time personal rather than professional, in being older. Things which would constitute a humiliation to a younger person are often dismissed as of little importance by older people. This applies especially to matters of discipline. A young person may be at the very stage of normal rebellion, when any discipline is looked upon as an attempt to keep him in a state of resented childhood. The older person will be more likely to look upon it as an amusing curiosity.

Miriam, the former secretary turned occupational therapist mentioned in the first chapter, did. Of her course at the School of Occupational Therapy she said:

'I think I was less impatient of the restrictions than

> younger people were. A lot of them had been at universities or boarding schools, where there were lots of young men. *We* stood up when the mistress came into the room. This didn't bother me at all. It was quite amusing.'

But the younger people objected to all the restrictions almost as a matter of principle.

> 'The first year, it was a bit like an extended boarding school,' said Miriam. 'We were harangued if we didn't turn up. That worried me less than the younger people. It was an amusing and entirely new way of life. It didn't do me any harm, whereas the young people were in a state of rebellion.'

Advantages with tutors

One comforting point was quite clear, from the experience of the people I talked to (even if they did not specifically mention it, or even consciously understand it). Anyone who goes back to school must realise that, though relations with other students may determine whether they are happy or not, it is the relationship *with the tutors* which is more likely to be crucial to their *success*. And here the older student, even if he has a difficult time personally, can have an important advantage functionally.

Two late-starters I spoke to, both women, made the point categorically. The first was Pamela, the woman who studied in the Commonwealth, and later in Britain, to become a doctor. She said it had been easier abroad than in Britain, because her fellow students had been a cosmopolitan group and had tended to accept her.

I then asked her whether it had been difficult for her, entering the medical college at the age of 38?

'I was about fifteen years older than most of the students,' she replied. 'Yes, it made problems for me, because at that time I was going home after lectures to wash nappies. It was jolly exhausting physically, but there was no prejudice at the university – I didn't really lack for the social field there. Obviously I didn't join in the Saturday night hops very much, but I used to go to school dinners and dances. I had my own social life with my husband. I think what was probably more important was that I was accepted by them – I didn't feel out of it. It was a very cosmopolitan group. There was an enormous number of European immigrants, a lot of Egyptians, and quite a few Eastern Europeans whose parents had come out immediately after the war. A couple of other girls in my year were born in concentration camps, so there was not an insular attitude. The fact that I was fifteen years older than most of the other students certainly posed no problems from the point of view of the staff. It made no difference to them. What I had taken on, I had taken on with my own problems to cope with myself. The attitude of the medical faculty was that they were my problems and it was up to me to deal with them.'

The attitudes she encountered when she got back to her British medical school – though she was quite happy there – did not have quite the same ruggedness.

'I think there was probably a little more antipathy from the English male students. I was with a curious group. At that time, there were two units a year going through. There was a main course of, I believe, 90 students, but there were 35 in my group. They were partly people who had taken the year off to do the BSc in either physiology or biochemistry plus, in my own case, the Cambridge group, which consisted of people who had done a second MB at Cambridge and were then doing their clinical work. Certainly I identified more with the Cambridge group, and that may have been because they were the odd-men-out.'

Pamela's social difficulties were mild: she had the support of her husband and she was old enough to keep her eye on the essential fact that it was her relationship with her tutors that really counted. The sheer physical strain of having a family and an education simultaneously was for her the far greater problem.

'I think the worst part was the six months' clinical I took abroad,' she said. 'I don't regard it as showing a disrespect to the British course, but the other course was much more rigorous, and I found that once I was on the clinical course, it was no longer eleven-week terms but all the year, with four weeks' holiday. I could go for about ten weeks and then I just had to take a day off, to sleep. Once I got back to England it wasn't so bad, or as demanding. I had time to think, which I see as an advantage. There was time to stand back and look at what we were doing. Abroad, there wasn't. I feel that I was very fortunate in having done the second MB abroad because I think I was far more rigorously equipped theoretically than my British colleagues were. But I think, particularly on the clinical side, you do need time to think. And I had that in Britain. I didn't have to get up at five each morning.'

Take humiliations early

The second woman to make the point that tutors could have a more direct rapport with older students was Sally, a former shorthand typist who became senior probation officer in a men's prison. She came to Britain as an au pair girl after the Nazis rose to power in Germany. She did youth work in Oxford for five years and was persuaded to qualify in social work.

> 'I would have been about 31 then,' she said. 'This was the time when qualifications for social work were becoming more important. I went to a two-year diploma course in Oxford and I couldn't get a grant, because I had no local authority: nobody who was responsible. So for the first year I did it part-time, still working at the youth organisation. For the second year I scraped enough money together by working during vacations. I would have been qualified by about 33 in social administration studies, which at the time was a pretty highly thought-of qualification. It does not exist any more. I was the first woman really to be appointed to after-care work with ex-prisoners . . . But one of the biggest changes for me was at the age of 31, when I decided to become a social worker, and the greatest impact was my two years at Oxford. That was the most awakening, in the way I was stimulated and interested. Most of the students were younger than me, but I wouldn't have taken to it better had I been younger. On the contrary, because I was older, I got much more out of it. I was very conscious of that. Some others were practically my contemporaries. All our tutors were conscious that we were much more responsive to learning.'

Sally was sure, too, that she had managed her transition to life as a probation officer in a prison better because she was then 42.

> 'I would say that to understand all the dynamics, and cope with all the conflicts, you need a certain degree of maturity. There are positive advantages to taking these things on later in life.'

If Sally had one regret, it was not that she took up study at a late age, but that she did not take the final step of going on a probation officer's course and establishing herself as a probation officer in academic terms.

> 'It was felt that to become a "real" probation officer, you should take the course. But on the other hand it was decided that I had a considerable lot of experience, so that any more training as a probation officer wasn't particularly valid for me. Although they would have liked me to have qualified as a probation officer, they didn't actually press me into it. I became a de-facto probation officer without actually going through the exam. Workwise, there was very little adjustment. I suppose the change was that I belonged to a professional body for the first time. And I think in a way I did make a bit of a mistake by being a little stand-offish, I suppose, and not taking the training, because that meant I wasn't really accepted by my colleagues for a long time, even though I was a senior by then. For years the probation service had not accepted that social work in prisons had a professional quality which the work of a probation officer demanded. It was looked upon as below par, below their standards. Sometimes it was implicit, and sometimes it was more or less openly said, "You really don't know what you are talking about because you are not a probation officer." That sort of thing.'

The message from Sally's experience is clear. It is usually better to subject oneself to the *passing* humiliation of formal instruction late in life than to subject oneself to the *continuing* problems brought about by not doing so.

CHAPTER FIVE: FINANCIAL STEP-DOWN

It would be ideal if every enterprising change of career were automatically rewarded with a higher income and standard of living. Alas, life doesn't always reward with cash. It may happen, but, as competition for high-paid jobs is fierce, the reverse is just as likely: a need to make do with *less* money.

Such a difficulty is not insurmountable in middle age. Many of the people I talked to pointed out that family responsibilities were usually declining by then. In any case, even if the change in the pattern of living means less money (so that the benefits are mainly psychological) there can still be very great advantages to life as a whole.

This applies especially where a major programme of formal learning, such as going to a university, is undertaken. There is no guarantee that such a course will formally succeed, let alone justify itself in financial terms. Albert's was such a case. His decision to go to university led to less money, not more. Nevertheless he did not regret it.

Albert is a Scotsman who left school at sixteen. After an uneasy time in marine engineering, often away from home, he wanted to try something else. He found he lacked qualifications, and that this restricted his choice. He became a full-time area organiser for a political party, but then funds ran low, the local party organisations had become stronger, and the area job was phased out. He was 36. Albert decided he wanted full-time education.

'People said to me, "You ought to get qualifications. Why don't you try evening classes at the College of Commerce? You get a grant and go full-time to the college." I went for two O levels and three Highers, or A levels, as they would be in England. I don't really think I found the study difficult, because I was interested. The real problem was the domestic situation: I had a wife and a son and a TV and what-not. To get detached from that was hard, but I could not honestly say I found study hard. Adaptation is tougher as you get older, but to a large extent this is compensated by the desire to do it; whereas when you are at school you don't want to do it. There is also the reaction, especially if you are among younger students, of finding you are giving as much as you are receiving. If you are doing an essay you can draw on so many possibilities, whereas you see younger people working on it with some difficulty. This is an important side of being a mature student. I think bringing them in is quite a valuable asset for schools.'

The evening classes equipped Albert to go to university. Here he did encounter problems, partly because of the questioning attitudes that went with his mature years.

'The first year,' said Albert, 'I read modern European history, English and moral philosophy, which I failed. This is something I was warned about. If you know what is necessary and regurgitate it, no one expects you to become a philosopher, and they are satisfied. However, if you are older, you tend to question, and this can be extremely difficult. My second mistake was that I didn't like the English literature course, so I had a verbal invitation to continue in English or history. I said, "I don't like your English course, so I will pursue my passion for history." If I had done all the course, I would probably have gone through, doing completely what they wanted, even if I didn't agree with it. But in fact I discovered too late that I had made the wrong choice, considered simply in terms of examination results, which have always been my bugbear. I can work at history for thirty weeks but I find it difficult to regurgitate it in one six-hour examination. Continual assessment would suit me better.'

In his second year, he failed two history examinations. That was one failure too many, when coupled with the previous failure in moral philosophy. He could have gone on, and re-sat, but he decided he simply could not face the examination again.

The conditions under which he was studying were far from ideal. He did a holiday job as a taxi-driver, making less than he had been earning in engineering; but it supplemented his university grant. It was during the following year that he failed the examinations, and decided that he could not go through it all again.

'I talked to my adviser in studies and saw several others about it,' said Albert. 'They said, "Do go back. All you have to do is just one examination." But I would not have got a grant to do the course again. I could have re-sat all the ones I had failed – British and European history – because by passing in one of these I would have been able to go back and continue into my third year. But I said no. There was the economic problem, which was very difficult.'

Albert simply carried on driving the taxi, but now full-time. Financially it was a come-down, compared with his previous career. There was the added psychological disadvantage that his university experience had been – viewed solely in terms of qualifications gained – a failure.

He assured me he had no regrets. Just at the time when

it seemed his university experience would be a total loss, he became involved in working on the first issue of a new magazine.

> 'The magazine came out just as I was beginning to descend into a feeling of complete loss. This has become increasingly important, and my university experience has been useful here. I do book reviews, and articles every month. It has given me a tremendous interest. I have no regrets about breaking off engineering, and I don't regret having gone to university – it was very useful. Working on my magazine articles, I see that, had I not been to university, I would not do things as I do them now. University teaches you to look at the evidence and not accept it at face value – that even the authority of print does not mean that something is true. Your tutor takes two pieces of writing and puts them side by side and shows you how they contradict one another. When you apply this later, it can be quite a revelation.'

Albert also found that his life had been enriched by the friends and contacts he made among students and staff of the university. He was able to visit the university and know he'd be remembered.

It would be misleading to suggest that Albert was content to let matters stand as they were when we talked. He said he would consider going back to university for a third year, but could do it only if he could find some supplementary occupation which took up less time than his taxi-driving, yet still produced a basic income.

> 'I would have to finish my classes by the end of each morning. That would be difficult, especially if I were doing three subjects. I don't know whether I would be able to do it on an informal basis. I have considered sitting-in on the class and being an

independent scholar, which is something I have come across. I doubt whether I could get a grant at all today.'

Albert obviously felt less sombre about all this than an onlooker might suspect.

'I have come down materially since I left engineering, yes. But this is secondary to the satisfaction which comes from my work on the magazine.'

Being a taxi driver would not be a comfortable proposition for many educated minds to contemplate. It is not a role which carries easy access to middle-class social life. Albert reacted by exploiting the humorous possibilities.

'When at forty you say, "I am a taxi-driver," they have no idea how to react. They can't adjust to this idea and it knocks them off balance. But I don't find it difficult to live with: it doesn't bother me. It was a disappointment to my parents that I got out of engineering and then became a taxi-driver. But then, they were of an older generation, and completely centred on engineering. This idea of change and doing an obscure job, so I can write, doesn't fit into their pattern. And I often wonder, if I *had* gone on and got a degree, what would I do then? So many qualify at teacher training colleges in the hope of getting a job as a teacher – and that is one thing I would never do, teach. What else could one do? They go through this great cycle, going to school themselves, leaving it to go to what amounts to another school, and then go on to teach others in another school. A fruitless process. I think my experience has been fruitful for me, in terms of opening my mind and in terms of satisfaction. I don't think of what I have done as being a permanent sacrifice.'

The Bar: risky hopes

Even if a mature man's time at university, and his professional training, are both technically quite successful, it does not follow that he will make more money than he would have done by staying in his old, perhaps unqualified, job.

This is especially so when becoming a barrister, a process which *is* open to spare-time effort. Partly because it is possible to study for the Bar in the evenings, it is an over-crowded profession in Britain. Without useful social and professional connections, a late entrant (even though he may be more intellectually satisfied than in his previous work) cannot count on a high, or even reasonable, income.

William, who went to college at the age of 27, got a social anthropology degree as a mature student, did a post-graduate year, and decided that unless he had a Doctor of Philosophy degree he would not succeed as an academic. He then went on to read for the Bar in his spare time while working as a journalist.

The result, he told me, was that he had gone without coffee because he and his wife couldn't afford it. He bought supermarket own-brand breakfast cereals because they were a few pence cheaper than the big brand names. His earnings as a barrister, at one time, would have caused any manual labourer to come out on strike. However, he still did not regret his change of career.

> 'When I left Cambridge,' he said, 'I didn't want to spend any more time on study. I felt tired. I wanted to earn my living. I was 31. I had met my future wife, and we were married the year before I did the post-graduate year. At the end of the day, what was

I going to do? Was I going to be a lecturer or assistant lecturer in some red-brick university? I decided not. I got a job working for refugees and then as a sub-editor on a newspaper. I was studying hard at night. We had money worries, and we remortgaged our house. That kept me going. I also borrowed money. My mother lent me some money, but she was not a woman of means, and I had to repay her. Somehow I got through, and I was called to the Bar.'

This was far from being the end of his financial problems. Newly called, he had to do his 'pupillage' – serve, in effect, an apprenticeship with a barrister of at least five years' experience.

'You are a dogsbody,' said William. 'You listen, you observe, you assimilate. In this way you attain practical experience of what it is like to be a barrister. In the first six months, you are prohibited from accepting any brief or representing anybody, so there is no question of earning any money during that time. In the second six months you are permitted to represent people. You may get an occasional brief if you are in what we call a criminal set, a criminal or common law set. You may get a brief to represent someone in a Magistrate's Court, but there isn't a lot of money in it. Certainly doing criminal work – which I wasn't – it is possible to do a remand in the Magistrate's Court. Just to go along and deal with your client as the case is put over to another date, maybe for a hearing, and maybe because the matter has to go to a higher court. That is the second six months. Then you finish your pupillage.'

What happened then, said William, was very much bound up with the problems of the Bar as a profession. A barrister was not allowed to enter a partnership. He must practice from prescribed chambers; he must have a clerk, who is a hybrid character – a 'combination of theatrical agent who normally gets ten per cent of your brief fees, a kind of father-confessor figure at his best, a keeper of receipts and records of monies received and, if he is doing his job properly, a looker-out to get you work.'

William, whose pleasant home was to be remortgaged a second time before he was finished, then added:

> 'That is the theory. Very often there is a difference between the theory and the practice. But the biggest problem at the Bar is accommodation. It is a profession apparently open to all the talents, but of course I knew it was going to be tough at the beginning. People used to ask me, "Do you have social connections with solicitors?" Because of course a barrister cannot accept a brief direct from a member of the public, it has to be from a solicitor. I didn't have any social connections with solicitors, but I had one or two old friends who encouraged me by sending me the occasional brief. But, as I say, the problem is accommodation.'

The theory, he said, was that if you were any good, at the end of your second six months, you made an application for a tenancy to the chambers where you had done your second six months' pupillage. The tenancy meant you had the use of books, and this was quite exclusive of any fee you paid to your clerk. What had happened in recent years was that it had 'all boiled up into an enormous bubble, which burst'. A lot of new universities had been set up, many with law faculties. In addition, polytechnics had been running law courses and there had been an enormous outpouring of people who wanted to go to the Bar. There was a certain glamour image – like the theatre – which was, in fact, contrary to reality. But it appealed to a lot of young people, because it was something you could do as an independent person, and because of its affinity to language and courtroom drama. It was one of the few areas left in modern society where an educated man could be a self-starter, without becoming involved in an institution. The problem was that you could only practice from prescribed chambers, and they were 'chock-a-block, simply full up'.

The result, said William, was that when one went into the chambers for the first year, in effect they told you: 'Well, whatever happens to you during the coming year, there is no hope here for you at the end of the road and you will have to move on.' One took that with a pinch of salt, thinking it was because they didn't know you or your capabilities. Then one found it was true (notwithstanding any merit one might have): there really was no room at the end of the year.

How do such barristers survive?

> 'If they are in a criminal or common law set, they do the hack work in the Magistrate's Courts, the work that the other tenants don't want,' said William. 'That can represent a whole day's work – and that is before deducting expenses. You are useful and you can be used. And you go on, and become what is called a "floater at the Bar". You float in the sense that you have got no permanent chambers. There are many floaters. Many people don't realise the Bar is a hierarchical profession. The fact is that, at the very top of the hierarchy, you have very good sets, whether they are doing criminal or commercial work: I mean in the sense of the quality of the personnel, the barristers, the clerking, the work-flow. At the Bar, rather like football, you have a first division, a second division and a third division. If you don't get into the first division – *and this is extremely difficult for a late-starter*, who cannot possibly understand it at the outset – you are at a disadvantage. I don't say this with any sour grapes or malice, just as a fact. The chances are that

> the man with ability won't get into the top set, because there simply isn't room, unless he has very strong connections. And to those who say the Bar is very much an old boy network, my answer is, "So was getting a job in the docks or the printing industry in Fleet Street." It works in exactly the same way. It isn't something peculiar to the middle class.'

At the time of our interview, William had two small children, had remortgaged his house for the second time, and was 'up to his ears' in debt. A number of solicitors were putting work his way as was his clerk, and he was appearing in Magistrate's Courts four times a week. But his 'life-saver' was teaching law, without which he estimated he would have drowned long ago, financially. He was teaching three nights a week at three different colleges. Teaching banking students, he might have a three-hour evening's work.

In one week, he had done six hours and had also had another teaching commitment, teaching Bar candidates, for an hour and a half.

William estimated that his earnings during the second six months at the Bar were about a tenth of what he had been getting on the newspaper. 'I would say in my second year, gross, I probably picked up at the Bar and from teaching just over half of what I was getting when I left the newspaper job.'

William did not admit to regrets on the financial side, but did acknowledge anxieties: the sort which are fairly common among men who have gone late to a profession in which long-standing connections are important.

> 'I worry every time I get a bill for the gas or the rates on this house. I worry when I go out on Saturday and do the shopping for my wife: I feel terribly guilty because I think I am being mean, in the sense that I have to watch every penny we are spending. I don't say we are on the poverty line, but I have to be

> careful about every penny we spend, because I am running an overdraft.'

House repairs tended to be deferred. When he sent his wife and children away for a holiday they did not go to a hotel but to a house they shared with a friend and his wife. William carried on working in London by himself. He also did some journalism when summer relief work was needed. I could not accuse William of empty vanity when he said: 'I sometimes get headaches, but I think my record proves I have tremendous powers of determination.' The new job had made him temporarily poorer but (as often happens) had paradoxically expanded his opinion of himself.

The commitment goad

Why don't people faced with an almost impossible struggle, after a taxing period of formal learning, fall a complete victim to despair? From three men I talked to, who all came late to the Bar, I gained the impression that the more they committed themselves, the more they felt they simply could not retreat. They had devised for themselves their own commitment goad. Some of their experience goes back many years, but is still relevant to more recent times.

> 'Did I ever lose heart? I didn't have much alternative to keeping on. Once you have put your hand to the plough, you have got to go on.'

This was Duncan, whose job as a district superintendent in the Indian Police came to an end, after the British withdrawal from the Empire. He was then at the most inconvenient age of 47.

> 'In my first year as a barrister I got nineteen guineas. The cost of the chambers was considerably more. I had my police pension, which was very small in those days. It was very hard going,' said Duncan. 'I probably began to be self-supporting when the Old Bailey rang up the chambers one morning and said if I was doing nothing would I come there and give them a hand in court. They were short of clerks of arraigns. I went on doing it after that, and became more or less permanently clerk of arraigns, the clerk who sits in court in front of the judge. I was never officially appointed to the job, but nevertheless I was doing it almost permanently. That must have been five years after I entered the job.'

Duncan was undoubtedly conscious of a great struggle to create a new life. He eked out his income by writing for law magazines and also wrote a book.

> 'Someone of that age has very little hope at the Bar,' he said at the home he had chosen for his retirement. 'The barristers' clerks don't like it. Solicitors' managing clerks don't like it. So unless you already have a reputation or some pull, you have to be very lucky to get work quickly. It wasn't until legal aid came in that one got bigger fees. I had been doing the job for three years before I earned enough to pay the expenses.'

Duncan's wife then gave her own memories of the struggle:

> 'He wore the same overcoat for twenty years. My mother-in-law had kept it back for him all through the war. It was a very disheartening period. He got very depressed, and didn't want to do much. I think he was disappointed that a lot of the things we used to have, we now couldn't have. We couldn't have a

car or holidays. The children went to any school we could find; but only one went to a state school. The others we managed to send privately, but they couldn't have any of the extras, music or elocution or anything like that. And clothes were always passed down: they started at the top and went down to the youngest.'

Eventually Duncan compromised. He retired from practising at the Bar at the age of 63, as he was becoming increasingly deaf, and took to farming.

Good and bad compromise

The instinctive realisation of when to compromise and when *not* to compromise is important. Only an unmarried person without friends, and setting no store by the value of social contact, can in practice push a career change to the bitter end, irrespective of the surrounding circumstances. Such a person would be an oddity.

A far more common mode of behaviour in an ambitious change of career is expressed in the phrase of the third man to become a barrister, Stephen, the ex-Fleet Street journalist: 'Cut your losses.'

Stephen's worst period was when he was qualified but had no money coming in. Like William, he was not able to stay on in the chambers in which he had been a pupil.

'There were possible opportunities in other chambers, but I wasn't prepared to stick it out any longer. Well, I suppose that wasn't entirely true. We did have some capital left, and we could have sold our house and moved into a less fashionable area: we could have done various things to raise money. But I felt it was like playing a game of cards. In a betting game, you are prepared to put so much on the table, then, if you have any sense, you cut your losses –

you don't go on playing in the hope you will reach the jackpot. That is my attitude. I cut my losses and I was lucky – I got a job with a firm of city solicitors in their tax department. It isn't usual, really, to move into a solicitor's office while you are a barrister, but it *can* be done. You have to become disbarred as a barrister, then you have to apply to the Law Society for acceptance as a solicitor. In my case the conditions were punitive, because they made me take all the solicitor's part-two examinations. But as the papers covered a lot of the ground I had already dealt with in the Bar exams, it wasn't too bad. I passed them, except for one paper, which I have still to take. Not many people follow this route because nobody who has just taken the Bar examinations wants to sit several more examinations for the Law Society. But I wasn't in the position to be choosy.'

Had his nerve faltered? Not at all, he insisted, it was simply money. 'Yes, you can make a lot of money at the Bar, if you succeed in it, but what good would that have done at the time, when taxation was so high?'

Stephen reasoned that if he had stayed at the specialist Bar, he could have looked forward to making quite a lot of money, but usually it takes three years at least before one can make anything decent.

'Well, think of three years at the rate of inflation which existed when I made this decision. That will eat your savings away, and so the *real* cost of sticking it out for two or three years was absolutely astronomic. I just wrote it off on that basis, and I don't regret it. I don't look upon my affairs, or life in general, as how I would *like* it to be; I just look at it as it *is*, and act accordingly . . . I am not making as much now as I would have done had I stayed in Fleet Street, but we make enough. We can manage *and things can only get better*, so I have no complaints on that score.'

Stephen's experience gives a clear idea of what constitutes a wise compromise and what constitutes a cowardly one. A wise one is not resented inwardly, which results in a course which is a tangible career change and, more importantly, opens up a path to continued progress in the future. Only retreat to a dead-end solution can legitimately be called a true defeat.

The values prison

Those who voluntarily choose a job with less money must compensate by managing their money better than they did before. It is the essential for a contented life. Most of the people in this situation that I interviewed agreed on the importance of this point.

Lewis, the stockbroker's clerk who became a probation officer, was especially emphatic about it when I asked him how he had adjusted to a lower salary.

> 'It meant organising my finances *much* better. I was very disorganised before, and I could run up an overdraft without worrying about it. I had one or two quite good holidays, and I used to eat very well. I would go out to restaurants perhaps three or four times a week, entertaining girl friends, people like that. I remember once I went into a restaurant and picked up the bill for the two of us – it was for £38. That was years ago, and it was a lot of money. I think it was ludicrous now. I just waved credit cards and that was it. I used to buy lots of clothes, three suits at a time.'

When he became a probation officer, things had to be different. His salary was then half what his earnings as a stockbroker's clerk had been at peak: allowing for inflation, much less than half.

'I was not married then, but many of the things I was used to were definitely out. Once I had got into social work, I don't think I ate out for about a year. I really cut everything down.'

When I asked Lewis if this had affected his self-esteem (a possibility that tends to hold people back from a change of this type), he said, 'No, I just adapted to a totally different way of life, with other values. I adapted to it quite well.'

The conclusion to be drawn from Lewis's experience is that a markedly different way of life, among new people, makes it easier to step down financially than one could easily imagine while still continuing the old way of life. The existing situation and standards can assume too much importance in one's reckoning, and become a prison.

The change of job broke the bars of one important human cage of Lewis's.

'When I thought I was going to make it financially, one of the things that did frighten me was that people who were well-off would think other people were after them because of their money. When I took a girl out, I wondered that. I met my wife when she was an ancillary worker, and neither of us were earning much money. I started chatting her up. I think she would probably have seen right through me if I had been in my former occupation.'

A decided human gain.

Licence to be poor

Robert, the former chartered accountant and management consultant who became a Church of England rector, argued that his business experience had enabled him to balance his personal books, and it was this ability that had made his new way of life acceptable. Also (as I saw it) he had acquired a sort of moral and social licence to be poor.

When he first thought of becoming a Minister, he was earning five times what he could expect as a parson. He decided against the move, because his children were still in the process of being educated. When he finally went on his ordination course, he managed to devote part of his time to consultancy jobs which produced handsome fees. It was only when he was ordained and moved out into his first job as curate, in a stockbroker belt, that the financial problems became acute. He then fully realised the need for strict budgeting if he were to adapt to the new way of life.

> 'We had a jolly nice house and we had to give it up. It did not really give me any pangs. We were very fond of it, but it was more of a wrench for my wife than for me,' he said. 'She was wholly loyal, so we moved into a house that was being pulled down. We were there for months and then we had to move into digs for five months while they were getting another house ready for us. It was one floor of an Edwardian place, which was very different, obviously, from what we had been used to.'

Their whole standard of living went down. Previously Robert had run a big car and his wife had driven a Mini. They went back to having only one car, a small second-hand Ford.

I asked Robert whether he still had financial problems.

> 'No. Being a chartered accountant, I have always balanced the books, and being a consultant I know about budgeting. Therefore I have done some strict budgeting. I was a member of a little luncheon club, but I gave that up. We also gave up our membership of the golf club, because that was too expensive. A

> lot of things were pruned away. But perhaps my wife could tell you better what sacrifices we had to make, and how we managed.'
>
> 'I would estimate' she said, 'that we more than halved our income at first. I couldn't have help for the house, but I didn't mind that. I was overjoyed at what my husband had done and I didn't see it as a sacrifice. We used to go to the wonderful chartered accountants' dinners and meet that type of person. All that went, of course. We could never have whisky in the cupboard. But, then, we are not really like that anyway. We have sherry for our friends, but we neither of us really like that sort of life. We are not the cocktail party types. We did not want to go in for vast entertaining. Our entertainment always has been, and still is, having friends in for a meal or putting up our friends or someone who is lonely for the weekend. Or people who are in trouble. We have never been the sort who want to throw parties and lead a madly gay social life. We have always hated it, really. As for food at home, one eats much more economically, of course.'

Robert's wife then made the crucial point from her own experience:

> 'Socially it didn't matter, even when we were very hard up in the early days. People knew we were the curate and his wife. We weren't *meant* to have anything.'

In other words, intelligent people, or people who need your company or reassurance, do not look down on you because you have little money – provided you are in a job which is *known* to carry little money. This gives you a *licence to be poor*. Earning relatively little in a profession known to be lucrative would impose the greater stigma.

Living with uncertainty

A smaller salary is much easier to live with if it is at least *assured*. New activities with an unpredictable income, or an unpredictable future, may impose a strain greater than the physical effects of lack of money.

This is indicated clearly by the experience of Anthony, the architect who became a visiting academic at two universities to develop his work on earthquakes and other natural disasters in the Third World.

Anthony estimated that by now he would be earning somewhat more had he stayed in architecture.

> 'My salary is high for a research secretary, because research is usually undertaken by younger people. But it is not the income level itself that worries me so much. It is its continuity – or, rather, its lack of continuity. It has meant that, when I was freelancing on my research, the money was totally uncertain from month to month. And, even when I was attached to a university, the future was not assured very far ahead. My two years at one university in particular were a dreadful reminder of what a short-termed existence one lives. No sooner have you been there for eighteen months than you have to think where your next opportunity is coming from. About two-thirds of my time was spent on wondering how my project was to get support. An academic's salary is sticky. I certainly did not make my move for the money.'

Anthony was very sure of what he wanted to do. He felt a strong moral compulsion as well as a careerist one. Anyone with less strong motives would be best advised to avoid such an uncertain way of life, even if it presented itself as an 'escape' from an existing and unwanted career.

The pension cushion

Taking an early pension may be a useful way of cushioning the low salary of a new career, though its perils in times of volatile inflation need careful thought.

Kenneth. who moved from the personnel department of a large company to the general secretaryship of a charity, at under half the salary, took this course.

> 'I took my pension straightaway, but it was obviously reduced because I took it very early. I did this to cushion the drop in salary while my youngsters still needed support. But I know it does mean that I am building up a deficit, as it were, for later on when that pension will be worth less than it should be. However, it doesn't worry me at all, because I realise it is a price that has to be paid. I am adequately provided for: if you live modestly, you don't need a tremendous amount. My house was three-bedroomed, detached and very comfortable, but in no way lavish. I have a car which I bought seven years ago, and I will have it for a long time to come. My wife drives it too – we don't have a second car. But I do not feel less of a man for these reasons. Although I have less money than I did, in fact I've got much more responsibility here. I have a very much heavier job.'

This reasoning may come naturally to a person with partly religious motives and with, possibly, a puritanical streak. Others might find that doing more work for less money causes them resentment rather than satisfaction, especially if they were unduly preoccupied with the thought that their wives were suffering because of their decision.

The known commitment

Paul, the former manager of a bank and a building society who moved into a charity providing accommodation for old people, said that when he made the move, he lost at least £3,000 a year on his salary. I said that it must have caused him much soul-searching.

> 'No, not personally, because – and this sounds terribly pious – I have never been terribly concerned with money. This may sound a stupid thing to say, but money doesn't have a very high place in my own personal life. It probably *has* to be important to my wife and she would probably say to me, "Do you think we can manage?" But I have always believed, more or less, in doing what you feel to be right, and would advise other people to do the same.'

Paul was living up to his fairly high income, with perks, at the building society. The house, detached with four bedrooms, had to go. It was replaced by a rented house in the country.

> 'With the balance of funds created by selling the house, we supplemented my rather reduced income,' said Paul. 'Also, with a rented house, one had a known commitment, if I can put it that way. It did come at the time when our last child was just finishing the final two years at university. I think the problem now is that, whereas I probably could have managed reasonably well when I made the move, inflation is now really causing charities to think very hard. Probably, in my own organisation, we will have to do something like rationalise the staff to keep the whole thing moving at the same salary levels. And so I think one is paying the financial price, although to some extent it is offset, because I have used part of the capital from the house. I am not ashamed to do that, really. I feel our total expenses are becoming less as our family responsibilities become less.'

In Paul's view, he and his wife could manage at a very simple level of existence. The ideal for him would be a very small cottage and a simple lifestyle, because from Monday to Friday he was personally completely absorbed in the job.

> 'So the price is really a different lifestyle. And I am conscious of the fact that it may have a worse effect on my wife than on me; she is the person who is having to pay for the job I am doing at the moment. She would probably spend more money on clothes and lead a rather less simple life otherwise. We don't go to the theatre and don't go to concerts as much as we used to do. We are almost developing into a sort of rural life. I suppose the compensation is that she is getting involved in such groups as the Women's Institute. But it is a slightly different emphasis, one that is less involved with entertainment and more involved with the domestic scene instead. From my own point of view, it is very good, When one spends the week touring the country talking to groups and so on, one just likes to get back into a shell, really.'

Judging from the mild experience of Paul and others, a man who felt – or was made to feel – that his wife was seriously cramped in her desired lifestyle would be at a serious disadvantage in adapting to a new career at a lower salary, however congenial he himself found it.

His chief strength in the change – his moral authority – would be undermined.

The social paradox

The final point that emerged from several job-changers is a comforting one. A reduced income may go hand-in-hand with what other people regard as an *increased* social status.

'The interesting thing about social work,' said Roderick, the refugee watchmaker who became a social worker, 'is the kind of status you are accorded. I am the same person, but in social terms I have changed: I have become middleclass. A silly example. Before I became a social worker, we did an exchange with some French children from a French school. The organisation concerned tried to match people as best they could, and we got the child of a garage mechanic. If that were *now*, I would get a teacher, or a civil servant, something of that sort. *I* haven't changed – I always had middle class kinds of friends when I was a watchmaker. But I am now in a different stratum of *The Guardian* readership scale. It just amuses me.'

CHAPTER SIX: RESISTING ILL-LUCK

Rosalie had just become head of the English department of a girls' school. She thought her career was comfortably mapped out until she retired at sixty. On one otherwise unexceptional day, she also thought her pupils were talking in softer voices.

Both assumptions were wrong. They could have been wrong even more tragically, but for her own willpower and capacity to adapt without self-pity: the two essentials found in all those people who somehow survive alive and kicking when they find themselves confronted by an adversity that may be physical, mental, economic, emotional or circumstantial.

In Rosalie's case, the misfortune was physical, as it is with a large proportion of people who are *forced* into a different way of life and career.

The first signs were not immediately alarming. 'It was ten years ago now,' said Rosalie, a tall girl with an open, good-natured face. At her flat, she sat with me directly in front of her and watched my lips carefully all the time.

> 'I was nearly 28. I was in the middle of a lesson at the girls' secondary school where I worked, when I noticed the children's voices were disappearing, getting fainter. So was my own voice. It didn't *seem* as if I were becoming deaf, just that everyone was becoming voiceless. After about an hour and a half, I heard nothing more. I thought, "How very odd." '

She saw her doctor the next morning. He said, 'You will have to give up your job.' The deafness, he said, would be permanent.

> 'He didn't know the reason,' said Rosalie. 'I still don't know. It didn't hurt or anything like that. It was as if I suddenly found myself in a glass box, or full of cotton wool. You could see everything that was going on, but there was no sound. My doctor said, after six months, that there was no hope for me.'

Rosalie was not conscious at the time of being upset about the state of being deaf itself.

> 'What affected me was my career disappearing, because I had never done anything except teach. At first all I could say was, "I don't know what else I want to do; I want to teach." '

The stunning nature of her affliction was slowly beginning to sink in. She had one major piece of luck: the local education authority were very patient with her, wouldn't accept that she had to leave teaching, and kept her on nine months' sick leave. They asked her if she would go and teach at an infants' school for blind or deaf children. Another teacher was going away on a training course to teach deaf children, and Rosalie thought she might take over her duties, so she went to the school. It was not a happy experience.

> 'I had never met a deaf person in my life. I couldn't lip-read very well. I had had all my teaching experience teaching girls, and some boys, aged between eleven and eighteen. I now found myself faced with a group of four- and five-year-old stone-deaf children. I hadn't had time to get used to my own deafness, so it didn't work out very well. I didn't even know how to teach normal children of

that age. I felt very bothered about not knowing what I should be doing. I would have been very happy to have *trained* to teach those children, but I wasn't allowed to train. Deaf people are not allowed to teach deaf children. Well, I think they may be able to now, because one or two people have. But the idea then was (and still is in many schools) that you must teach deaf children to learn to talk, and if you can't hear yourself, you can't teach them. So I gave it up. I only did it for three weeks.'

This was after a six months' break following the start of her deafness. It disappointed her. She had had a holiday, hoping that some hearing might return, but it didn't. During the sick leave, she had got herself a contract to write an article, for an encyclopaedia, on the modern novel. This meant she had to get down to some solid reading, which gave her something to do at a time when she badly needed it, even if the money was not enormous.

The education authority came up with another idea. They said, in effect: 'Tell us what you want to do. If you want any training, we will give you a grant to be re-trained. What about being a librarian?'

They made a job for her, extra-establishment, as a librarian-clerk. It was a generous move, but it was an embarrassment. Rosalie found the situation difficult because it seemed, on the surface, such a sensible idea; and yet she felt it was wrong for her. Her unhappiness deepened.

'I was stuck in the cataloguing part of the library, and I wanted to work with *people*. There wasn't really a job for me to do, so I found myself in the cataloguing department, typing indexing cards with two fingers because I couldn't type. In the end I asked them to let me become unemployed, because I was all mixed up about what I did want to do. Initially they were paying me my teacher's salary, but by the end of my nine-month sick leave I was receiving less. Even so,

I was still getting quite a lot of money, which I felt terribly guilty about, because I wasn't doing anything. I thought that if I became unemployed I would be less drain on the State, and could spend my time looking for things to do. It is quite funny now, looking back on it.'

It did not seem funny at the time. She got into a 'dreadful state' about it: the deafness, the career uncertainties, the sense of guilt.

'I wondered if my deafness was hysterical, as it didn't seem to bother me, in itself, at first. I got in touch with a psychologist I knew. He was working at an eye, ear and throat hospital and took me in for a thorough examination. I had two days of electrographs and so on and ended up with them saying, "Yes, you *are* deaf; it is not hysterical. We don't know why." It sorted out that question for me.'

Other factors were not so easily sorted out. She was living on her own, and this produced enormous complications. She could not answer the telephone or ring anyone up, nor could she hear if anyone knocked on the door. If she knew people were coming, she had to sit at the window, waiting for them. She would wait for hours for the gas man to turn up, not daring to leave the window. Rosalie then knew nothing of bells with flashing lights, and knew no one who was familiar with the problems of the deaf and how they could be solved.

It was fortunate that she lived in a small town. She was secretary of the local Workers' Educational Association, and thought she ought to give it up, but the members asked her to carry on. She was relieved, because she needed things to make her feel useful, and she did not want to move.

'It was difficult enough, coming to terms with things there, without moving elsewhere as well. I was going to lectures and people were making notes for me. I think I was very lucky that it was a small place. I was the young Miss who had taught at the High School and who had suddenly become a nine-day wonder. Everyone knew about it. Some people were a bit embarrassed, but I tried to go out to *them* and not let them be embarrassed by it, so they were very quick in learning how to help me. I felt I was being quite useful. Any unemployed woman is useful, in the sense that there are old people about who need tasks done for them, and that kind of thing. I might just go and see them and do shopping for them, something like that.'

She wrote to the editor of a local newspaper and he gave her a little book reviewing to do each month. Technically, she was unemployed and remained so for ten months. During that time, she did some correspondence course teaching for a college, and tried to come to terms with her various problems as best she could.

'I don't know how long it took me to lip-read,' she said. 'At first I couldn't pick it up at all, but then I learnt it very quickly. I didn't have any formal lessons, I just got on with it. I started to teach myself Italian, and brushed up my French. The only idea I could think of was perhaps getting a job in educational publishing. Therefore, more languages would be useful; typing would be useful. I spent an enormous amount of time writing round and getting nowhere. Then I applied to a corporate body as a proof-reader. It was not so much that I wanted to do proof-reading, but it seemed a step towards something to do with publishing. I also felt the time had come when this was the right thing to do. My parents were living about twenty miles away, and I had friends in the area, too. But obviously I couldn't get a job where I was, over 100 miles from London. I had to move out anyway, probably to London.'

The corporate body mentioned two vacancies, one for a proof-reader and the other for an information analyst. She asked for, and got, the information analyst's job. It involved a study of companies who were tendering for contracts, and the changing market in commodities – from essential oils to tin. She reported to her employers on the price fluctuations that it was important for them to know. What had happened, was happening, and was likely to happen, to Chilean copper? Was it likely to be nationalised? What would be the effect of the ending of a war on wool prices?

Rosalie went into the job for a trial period of six months, and stayed for two and a half years. She quickly gained rises in status and salary so that, ironically, she was eventually earning considerably more than she had as a teacher. Also ironically, she was dissatisfied and rather bored. She had not yet adapted her conscientiousness to her disablement and new circumstances.

> 'It is difficult to say whether I was really better off financially, because it was very expensive, living in London. My London flat cost me three times what I had paid when I lived outside London. I was bored with my job in London. Again, I think I hadn't really come to terms with my deafness, and the way other people worked. I had gone from school to university and back to girls' schools. Most of us there were unmarried, and I was very dedicated. It was very odd to go into a situation that was so much more relaxed, and where you weren't always busy. Often there wasn't much to do. I think I would quite like it now, but then I thought it was awful, a terrible waste of public money. I think I must have been an absolutely poisonous colleague, sitting in judgement on everybody!'

I asked Rosalie when she thought she had finally come to accept her deafness emotionally as well as intellectually.

She said it must have been seven or eight *years* after she had gone deaf.

In the meantime, she worked on, having little social life in the evenings. She spent most of them doing her correspondence teaching, 'because it was something else to think about.'

> 'It was difficult to think of other jobs that I might do. What other qualifications could I get? Should I do some researching on seventeenth-century literature? All the time I was not accepting that part of my life was finished.'

Eventually she found the beginnings of a solution by allowing herself to be guided by outside circumstances: a not uncommon formula for 'breaking out' when no escape can be found by sitting down and thinking deliberately about it. In taking her flat in London, she had moved near to where her former post-graduate tutor lived. The tutor's husband died and she decided to move out of London. Rosalie gave up her job and moved out with her.

It was now that she found the job in publishing that had eluded her in the nominally more likely ground of London. A small publishing firm gave her sub-editing work to do, processing submitted material for printing. Though the firm was a 'cottage industry', and though her salary was cut to a third of what it had been with the corporate body, she found she enjoyed the work more. She felt it might lead somewhere, and it did.

> 'I didn't mind because I was busy, and I lived with my former tutor so my living expenses went down. Also I think I was very realistic in this sense: I knew that what I was getting was not the rate for the job. On the other hand, I knew if I wanted to get anywhere in publishing I had to prove I had experience, so it came in handy. I did the job for a

> year, and then I took on some editorial freelance work for various publishers. I got a commission to write a specialist encyclopaedia. It was in four volumes, and they wanted me to do the third one. My old tutor regularly wrote an article on their subject for an encyclopaedia, and they thought it would be a very good thing to do another one, but my old tutor didn't want the job. So they asked if I would like to take it on, and I said, "Yes, please".'

It was not, in the end, work that gave her an acceptance of her condition. It was the premonition of the possibility of an even greater personal disaster.

Something began to go wrong with her eyes. It seemed as if she might be going blind, as well as being deaf.

> 'I didn't like this at all. I thought, "I can cope with being deaf, but blindness! – No, thank you!" It was a false alarm, but I didn't enjoy it very much at the time. It only lasted a month, perhaps, before I managed to see again. I went to a neurologist. It wasn't anything very much at all, apparently. What happened was that I was having a set pattern of spots. The occulist thought this was horribly significant of something, and that I ought to get something done about it, but as it turned out it wasn't very serious. I somehow think that made me accept my deafness – really accept it. It was only superficially that I had accepted it very rapidly.'

She now began to think not merely of how deafness could be accepted but – a very signficant step in her career – how it could be *used*. This was when she started to think about becoming a social worker for deaf people, including those who had been born deaf, and whose affliction was worse than her own.

She totted up the positive side of her personal score card: working with people was what she liked; she had a good education; she could communicate fairly easily with young people; she knew what it was like to be deaf. Even so, she sought objective checks on her *own* assessment of her assets.

> 'I tried to discover what other people thought about this. I had always thought that if I didn't teach I would do social work, but when you are deaf you are unlikely to be given the chance to do ordinary social work. Everyone said, "Yes, it is a very good idea." So I applied for training, and got accepted. I finished the general part of the course at a London polytechnic, which seemed at the time to be the only place in Britain which made provision for deaf people on social work courses. The course lasted two years.'

The course involved inevitable, and sometimes unforeseen, problems. They were faced by others as well as herself. According to Rosalie, the administrators of the course found it difficult to select practical work in which they could 'take the risk' of testing deaf people, 'because if you are in social work, you can hit the headlines if you're not careful.' The deaf students had an interpreter at lectures. The translation was literal, so that if a lecturer said 'Um' or 'Er', the interpreter said it as well. There was a born-deaf student on the course, which enabled Rosalie to make a useful comparison.

> 'He was only 23. Just being *older* than he was helped. And I had a lot of academic background behind me, so the theoretical part was easy. It was very helpful for both of us, I think, to figure out the other's contribution.'

She found that the biggest difficulty was being 'labelled' as a deaf person, because there were only the two of them in a course of eighty, and they sat right at the front with their interpreter.

'It made me realise for the first time what it is like to be labelled by society, like a parcel. It made me understand how it felt to be in a wheelchair, for example. This is very useful. In my job as a social worker it helps to know what this sort of thing is like.'

Rosalie's obvious dedication inspired her new employers, a London borough, to give her a year in which to do further specialist training before she started work for them as a social worker among deaf people. She had asked for it, and with 'almost unprecedented generosity' they had agreed to pay her while she did her year's further training. Rosalie was still on the course at the time of our interview.

'It is half practical work and half theory. For the theory, we have lectures on the problems of hearing parents in bringing up deaf children, or in deaf parents bringing up hearing children. Most deaf people have hearing children and most deaf children are born to hearing parents. They also deal with communication and sign language, and the technical problems of what you do when a deaf person is having, say, a medical examination. How you communicate such questions as "Do you wheeze?" to a person who has never heard what a wheeze is? Then there is fourteen weeks' work in the social agencies for deaf people, and six weeks' work in a psychiatric unit.'

How do you assess whether a person is tolerably happy or not? Any guess may easily be insensitive. Rosalie was living with her old tutor, who was able to answer the telephone for her and talk to her in a way she could lip-read. She had the promise of a job that would interest her and convince her that she was capable of doing objective good in the world. But her social life was surely bound to be more barren than that which a woman of her age with full hearing would be comfortable to accept?

'It's frustrating in that, if I could hear, I could be going to concerts, or evening classes, or that sort of thing. I wouldn't say it actually *upsets* me. I am doing a correspondence course in logic, and am thinking about doing a doctorate in the subject, to keep me stretched. I have become a committee woman with a vengeance. If it is a small committee, where there are two of us who are deaf, then the chairman's wife will usually sit between us and make notes for both of us. I joined the council for various official bodies dealing with disablement. Sometimes, some of the other members, who are experienced in working with deaf students at the Open University, will interpret for me. Otherwise one of the secretaries makes notes for me or I lip-read, but that can be a bit tricky in a big group.'

In filling her life with activity, Rosalie escaped some of the worst regret at her shortage of social life. Her manner, when I met her, was always cheerful. Eventually I was encouraged to ask her the necessary question which could so easily sound completely insensitive: had her affliction given her any positive benefit as a human being? I was intensely relieved when she laughed.

'I was an absolute prune before. It is difficult to know how much the difference was due to my becoming deaf and how much it was because I was growing older anyway. There is a big difference between 28 and 38, isn't there? At 28 I was a classic old-fashioned schoolma'am: very shy, terribly self-conscious. I realised very quickly that *other people* were going to be self-conscious because I was deaf. If I wanted any social life I had to make other people feel comfortable, and not worry about what *they*

> thought about *me*. That was a good result of becoming deaf; I think it added something.'

There was also, she said, the experience of the other jobs, which she would not have had but for her deafness. She hadn't enjoyed many of them at the time, but she had learned a lot. It was useful to know how industry worked and what it was like to spend one's working life in an office. It gave her more insight into other people, which would be useful to her in her social work.

Many disabled people maintain that even if their disability were to be magically removed, they would stay in their new life rather than go back to the old one: disablement can often be a pointer to undiscovered parts of the working self. Rosalie was such a case.

> 'It is very difficult to know what I would do now if I got my hearing back. I think it would drive me round the bend to start with, because of the noise. I expect I would go on with what I am doing. I am not sure about going back into teaching; if I did, I think I would probably want to train other people to help deaf people get a better education. I don't feel like spending twenty years as a grassroots social worker for the deaf. This is not because I think it is a bad job or anything like that, but because there are few people of my frame of mind who are deaf. I think I might be able to stand on a platform and talk to people about the problems of disabled people. If I were to stand on a platform and say, "If I shout at you, it is because I don't know I am making a noise, so please point it out," it would have enormous punch. I think there is more awareness of the deaf and their problems, but I would like to do something not just about these but also the general problems of disabled people. I have my own views, which I should like to get across. At these special schools, so much time is spent making deaf children make noises

which they call talking, but which no one will ever understand. Why not teach them in signs to start with and *then* teach them to read, and give them an education?'

Rosalie was able to bubble over with new ideas and to say, with every appearance of sincerity, that she was a richer person for her disability and that she was 'glad' it had happened: the original mountain she had to climb was nearer to being a molehill. She now had qualifications in a new job, whereas at first her *previous* qualifications were paradoxically her biggest stumbling block in changing her career.

> 'Part of my problem was my degree in English. I had a career as a schoolma'am, a degree in English and no other qualifications. People felt, "We must pay her a lot if we take her on because she has been head of a grammar school department," so they thought twice about it.'

The double blow syndrome

It would be merciful if physical and emotional handicaps could always be faced separately. In practice one is often bound up with the other: sometimes they are cause and effect. This can produce a chain of misfortune which can be very difficult indeed to deal with. It can nevertheless be turned to positive account, beaten, or at least forced to an honourable draw.

I found the willingness of Hester to discuss her own situation quite extraordinary. The mere recital of it, I would have thought, must have been painful; but like the other people I spoke to, she was actively glad to talk, finding it helped her make sense of her varied misfortunes, her pain, and – more importantly – her hopes for the future.

On top of disablement, Hester encountered divorce – and divorce in the most painful circumstances: those in which she felt herself to be supplanted while helpless and unable to fight back. When I knocked at the door of her bungalow, she opened the door herself.

She was in an electrically-propelled invalid chair. It was the first interview I had sought for this book, and I was less composed than she was, fearing she would mistrust my interest and find insensitive many questions I might put to her. She guided me to an armchair, using her own invalid chair to do so, and then drove out into the kitchen to make me a cup of coffee. The superficial impression I had gained was of a markedly self-composed woman of middle age, with carefully tended hair, neat inconspicuous clothes, a businesslike manner and the slight trace of a North Country accent to reveal her origins. Her husband had believed that all the really shrewd members of his profession gravitated South, so that is what he had done. He settled down quite well.

For Hester, the move did not turn out to be so fortuitous. Eighteen months later, she contracted poliomyelitis, and was in hospital for over a year. 'Life was rather rough then,' said Hester.

This was certainly no overstatement. The couple had fostered a little boy, then Hester became pregnant and it was at this point – three months into her pregnancy – that she contracted polio. Her husband struggled to keep the fostered boy at home, because the child had already had several changes of home and had suffered accordingly. The husband battled on with the help of various friends and relatives who came in to help. After over a year in hospital, Hester went home, but she had to have a housekeeper because she was still almost totally paralysed and could not do any housework.

At this stage, the reality of what had happened to her still had not fully penetrated: it did not occur to her that she would spend the rest of her life in a wheelchair. She was still only in her thirties. She began trying to do small things, such as wash up or peel a potato. 'I looked upon it as an exercise, really. I never really *thought* about the disability at all.'

She coped like this, as a housewife, until one of the children was in his teens. It was at this point that she took a job, beginning what was to be a period of enhanced disappointment and frustration to her.

> 'The boy was getting rather difficult in his teens,' she remembered. 'There were boys next door who seemed to be allowed to have everything they wanted. Our boy used to come along and ask if he could have this and if he could have that. And we said no, we couldn't afford it. I got so sick of saying, "We can't afford it, we can't afford it," that I thought eventually I might be able to get a job. We always needed money to help with the house, which was expensive, and we didn't have a lot of money to spare. This started me off trying to find work.'

Her first job was as a ledger keeper in an electrical firm. It was a part-time job and lasted a year. In the meantime, she had done welfare work for fellow sufferers and had acquired an electric vehicle. As she lived among steep hills, it could not take her very far, but at least it got her out of the house. When she got the job, her husband bought her an automatic-gear car which she managed to drive to the factory. After a year, she was told that a girl who was employed full-time would be doing her work in future, and was asked to leave. She then got a full-time secretarial job with a firm near where she lived. This too was to lead to disappointment.

> 'I was secretary to the marketing manager, and felt as though I was really getting somewhere. I worked like mad! I was up at six to drive down the road to the factory, and I really enjoyed it. I got on very well

there. I was with them for just over a year, then they amalgamated with another firm and moved. I was made redundant and was unemployed for nine months. The employment exchange were trying to find me jobs, searching high and low around this area. If they came across the right job and the employer said, "You sound ideal", you could bet the job would be upstairs or something like that.'

This phase of frustration ended when she got a job as secretary with an organisation connected with health in the South of England. She got on very well with her office boss, but not long afterwards came a major reorganisation. Her office boss applied for a job with the same organisation in a different town and offered to take his secretary with him if this were possible. One look at the map convinced them both that it would be out of the question.

By this time, Hester's misfortunes were compounded. She was separated from her husband.

This came about because she herself had suggested to her husband that he needed some outside activity to relieve the strain of looking after her. This was Hester's version of the break-up:

'I suppose I am a self-reliant character, within limits. I don't think that made our marriage less satisfactory than it could have been – we were very happy, as far as I thought. My husband had been absolutely marvellous all the time I had had polio. He had made life more and more easy and enabled me to be increasingly independent, by having a car and things like that. I said, eventually, that he ought to have some outlet other than being tied to the family all the time, so he went to evening classes for three or four years. We had other friends who went to these classes as well. There was another couple who went along, then the husband left the classes, his wife became friendly with my husband and after that . . . I didn't learn about it until the following year, but apparently she was meeting him in London, off the train here, and that sort of thing. It hit my morale for a long time. I think if my daughter hadn't been around, *I* wouldn't have been around any more. I felt my life was absolutely shattered, that all the struggle in getting over polio had been wasted, that it had come to nothing.'

The job Hester had at that time was not enough: she wanted 'a career job I could really work at, so that my mind was not worrying about other things.' She wanted to come home feeling she had done a good day's work, because she might then be able to cope with the rest of her life. She found that her social life largely disappeared, because her friends largely disappeared – 'even people from the Church.' She felt especially let down by this defection.

'I told the Minister I had lost faith, not in God, but in the Church; in people, rather. I don't think of God as a person, but I think one is surrounded by Something, a presence that just takes care of you, really. But as far as the Church itself went, in a sense I felt let down by them. As soon as my husband left, not a soul came near. At the time I couldn't have gone to church, because it was an effort to get into the building. Anyway, I knew darn well I would have just burst into tears. That happened a lot of the time. Everyone else was shattered and surprised as well, because someone once likened my husband and I to a couple of carthorses that always pulled together in everything we did. Yes, the woman was younger.'

Gradually she came to terms with the reality of her new emotional situation, enhanced by career difficulties.

'It took some years,' she said. 'I thought about things an awful lot. There was a new minister at the church, and perhaps that helped. I came to terms, I think, by looking at it in this way: my husband had done all this work for me, looking after me and the children during my disablement, and a time had come in his life when he should be free to do what *he* wanted, without being encumbered by a wife who couldn't get around – although, as the children were getting bigger, I could probably have got around a lot more. I thought that, perhaps, it was his turn to do something completely different. But it still wasn't easy.'

While she did her best to cope with this emotional turmoil, the difficulties of adapating herself to different sorts of job continued. The problems were intertwined.

The town her boss was moving to was nearer to where her husband was now working. She was tempted to move with the boss, in the hope that it might help her re-establish her marriage – at this point her husband was still saying he might come back to her and their daughter.

It was probably a measure of Hester's essential character – one of self-reliance – that she decided against this move. Instead, she stayed where she was and fought out her own problems from there.

She was asked to become secretary to a different functionary, and was with him for eighteen months before he left to work for another organisation. She worked for another man, then doubled for him and another official, which did not seem a very satisfactory arrangement.

Hester, on top of her other troubles, was now beginning to experience what has persuaded many people to a change of course: the *musical chairs situation*.

It is not uncommon in large organisations, especially among secretaries. A large number of women I spoke to who had been secretaries said that one of the most frustrating parts of the job was the feeling that they were not players in the game, but only the shuttlecocks, to be knocked around to suit other people's convenience. In the case of Hester, plainly a strong-minded woman, the condition was especially intolerable.

> 'That is how it went on, not being involved, really involved, in the work. Some of the bosses dash off to do their own thing and don't leave behind clear instructions, so that if anyone rings up and asks where Mr So-and-so is, you have to say, "I'm sorry, I don't know." This is an unsatisfactory situation. It was possibly part of working in a large organisation. I can't say I liked working in a bureaucracy. Then I had a new boss, and he would give me a page full of notes that would keep me busy all the week. That is what I liked, as he would just leave me to get on with it, and everything would run smoothly. He had to organise a big seminar once and he just said to me, "Right, see what you can do with this." I loved doing it, because I like organising things. I wanted to be central to my boss, to leave him to do the main things while I did the nitty-gritty. But then I had the feeling that he was not going to stay very long. There was a new personnel officer, and if your face didn't fit, you would be squeezed out – that sort of thing. He came to me and said did I know that my boss was leaving, and that I wouldn't have a job.'

Sometime before this crisis, Hester had decided that musical chairs was not an acceptable way of life.

> 'When my husband left, I wanted a job as a *career*. Something that was interesting, and that I could enjoy. Whereas in the past few months, I had trailed into work and trailed home again and thought, "What's it for?" Just for the salary at the end of the month, which I felt I hadn't earned, anyway.'

Her new life and career was in fact sparked off both by the break-up of her marriage and by the frustrations of bureaucratic musical chairs.

When she had first lost her husband, she had had the thought (which she insisted was not so much morbid as poetic) that she would like to be buried next to her grandfather in a small village churchyard in the North of England, where her ancestors had been born.

> 'The countryside was so beautiful. I said to my daughter how wonderful it would be to be laid to rest there, when one's life was finished. It was a *pleasant* thought, actually. We went up there for a holiday and afterwards I wrote to a man I knew through the church and said I might consider moving up there.'

It was her divorce which made the move possible. She was advised that the area she was moving into would not be easy for a disabled person; she replied that, being disabled, life was not easy wherever she lived. She was sent an advertisement for a bungalow in the area she wanted – one which happened to have been built for a disabled person. It had slopes instead of steps and was made with wider doors to enable a wheelchair to be manoeuvred in and out more easily. 'I said to my daughter that this was it. I had to have it.'

The bungalow was to provide a solution to both her emotional and working problems. She had always been keen on looking after people (she had at one point been an officer of an association for disabled people), and she had always been keen on cooking. The threads came together (as they sometimes do in the case histories of people who have made radical alterations in their mode of life) gradually but conclusively. She decided to open the bungalow as a bed and breakfast establishment. A male friend of hers who had driven her up to look at the bungalow in the first place (*insisting* that she looked at it), said that he would go up to that part of the country with her and help her run the bed and breakfast business.

Hester emphasised that she had not consciously planned any of her new way of life. But, to me, it did seem that an unconscious plan was visible: one that would free her from old memories and open up the possibility of new working and emotional experiences.

> 'It seems to be one of those miracles you think could never happen. I had not even thought that an interest in my ancestors, and where they came from, was an attempt to find myself. I had accepted that my life was going to be a hard one, and a struggle until whatever time it was going to end. But all of a sudden, it miraculously changed. Whether it is something in fate, I don't know. I had no fears or hesitations about the move, none at all.'

To an outside observer, it might seem that Hester's change was not due to fate so much as due to a steady progression towards the things that made an instinctive appeal to her: a business, albeit small, in which she could be a prime mover and not a functionary at someone else's beck and call, and a relationship in which she could be a dominant partner.

I asked her whether she would have been a secretary in the first place but for her disablement.

> 'Possibly not,' she said. 'I like organising and planning things. I must know where I'm going. Possibly I wouldn't have accepted secretarial work if I hadn't been disabled. I have been as happy as a sandboy when I have gone for weeks without seeing my boss.'

Hester's case illustrates the main danger with both physical and emotional misfortune: it can obscure the basic human identity of the sufferer, and make it that much more difficult to find an acceptable course. To me, having talked to her for two hours, it appeared that Hester had conquered her difficulties, in so far as it was humanly possible to do so; *not* by being a passenger or plaything of 'fate', as she herself seemed to think, but because she had been prepared to follow her instinct for what might be right for herself. Her success showed the potent effect of tentative self-exploration, combined with steely willingness to *act* deliberately and consciously on the fruits of it.

The delinquency barrier

There is one form of hardship which can be more tenaciously crippling to future hopes than even physical and emotional turmoil combined. In some cases it may spring from them. It is delinquency.

A non-delinquent may reach the age of thirty or more before what other people expect, and do not expect, of him becomes fixed for him by his known working role, whether he likes that role or not. In the case of a person who has got on to the wrong side of the law, the restricting reputation, which can make change so difficult, may solidify much, much earlier.

It is possible for the chains to be firmly in place before the age of twenty, let alone thirty. In such cases, effective 'middle age', and a set pattern of life, may occur before the person has lived a quarter of a century. Escape is then difficult.

Fortunately, escape is not completely impossible. Yvonne's case was an illustration of this, combining (in the factors that led to a wasted life) crime, lesbianism and alcoholism. She was over the worst of her difficulties when I met her, a heavily-built woman of 36, with a forcefully cheerful manner and intelligent smile readily on call when discussing her past shortcomings. She was a student at a women's educational establishment, had stopped drinking and had acquired a stable emotional relationship.

At fourteen, and for the next few years, the apparent tranquility in which I later found her would have seemed impossible. It was at the age of fourteen that she abruptly left her grammar school because of her delinquency and went to a girls' secondary school. She left that at fifteen. This is her own estimate of herself at that time.

> 'I was a delinquent. I was anti-social. I had home problems. I played truant. I didn't feel like other children. So I left school at fifteen and just did what I could. I tried clerical work, a little factory work, the Forces. My problem was lack of stability. I couldn't get on with people: I always felt at odds with them, and gave them up. I think it was the conflict at home, really. My mother died when I was little and my father married a middle-class lady. *We* were essentially working class. I think that, with the introduction of certain values into the home, I had a tremendous conflict. I was separated from working-class children and I couldn't integrate with middle-class children, so I was in a cleft stick. I think that contributed to my problems.'

She did not blame other people for her sense of isolation, which was to make her adaptation to useful intellectual effort so difficult.

> 'It was more a case that I was marvellously acceptable to other people, but I wasn't acceptable to *myself*,' she insisted. 'Now I have some middle-class values, but I also have some working-class ones. I would think I am pretty classless – I can mix easily with anyone. But at that time, I just lacked confidence: I had a big chip on my shoulder. One day I might go into work, feeling particularly sensitive, and have to do something I didn't want to do, and I would say, "Oh, —— it!" And off I went. I think in the Forces it was the same. I was a good athlete and

everything, but it wasn't big enough to hold me. I went absent without leave and I had relationships they didn't approve of, and I was just terribly unstable, I think. They were homosexual relationships – I was worse then. The Forces had rejected me. For the first time, *I* had been rejected. I went from bad to worse, and completely dropped out. I didn't drop in again until I was 25.'

Yvonne said that she had been convicted of several offences, including stealing and 'various offshoots of it.' She had also started drinking heavily.

'Generally, I was a social misfit. The stealing was really how I came to drop back in. It was only when I was *forced* to stop that I could really come to terms with myself and society. I was in a woman's prison on remand and I had a drink problem, quite a bad one. They thought I might reach about thirty years old, and that would be my lot. No – they thought I would be dead long *before* I was thirty. I was claustrophobic, I might add, and prison nearly drove me mad. But the psychiatrist in prison asked me if I believed in God or prayer and I said, "Well, I used to when I was young." And he said that there was a convent that specialised in the treatment of women – alcoholics and addicts – and would I like to go? I thought anything was preferable to the prison, so they put me on a conditional residence at the convent for six months, and then they imposed another six months because I was still quite unstable. But from there, I have progressed. I think that in the year in that convent – where they were particularly kind and rather spoon-fed me, and understood my problems – I came to understand that my problems were not unique and could be shared. I still couldn't come to terms with homosexuality, but they encouraged me tremendously.'

The convent arranged work for her when she left. It was domestic employment, of a residential kind, and she was was kindly treated. After six months of it, some people in the same locality offered her a home.

> 'That was a start. For three years, I kept going in and out of jobs. I took a course in professional skills connected with commerce, and got through that, but still I couldn't stick, I couldn't feel quite right. I was always working, wherever I went. I was always regarded as a very good worker, but I used to get very depressed and feel inadequate. I think this went on until I was 28. And then, suddenly, I took a job as a clerk and I stayed there seven-and-a-half years. I worked hard and was promoted twice. It was a tremendous rehabilitation and growth programme, really. I was also accepting the homosexuality. I didn't quite accept it until I was in the late twenties, because I couldn't equate it with the sort of moral beliefs I had – which came from conditioning, anyway. Then I began to accept it and I think I came to accept other people too: I wasn't frightened of them any more. I think the two things went together. It was a gradual growth, accepting the one thing and accepting people as well. By then I was nearly 34.'

It was at this point that she thought another change was due. She had always regretted her shortage of formal education, brought about by the fact that, although quite bright, she was always playing truant.

In a newspaper Yvonne saw an advertisement for a college, and enrolled for a two-year course on social service. She regarded it as a matter of broadening her horizons, understanding things she had always wondered about, and generally integrating with society. Eventually, she said, she would like to go on to university and take a degree in politics and sociology. After that, she didn't know.

Yvonne is one of those who is sure she made a much better student in her thirties than she would have done in her teens and twenties.

> 'I couldn't have done it then. Perhaps I would have had the intellectual ability, but not the *stickability*. I would probably have regarded it as rubbish, anyway. I would have had a mistrust of academic things: I had a mistrust of everything. I didn't differentiate.'

Had her problems given her anything of positive advantage, or were they all on the debit side?

> 'I think the advantage is that it has made me more tolerant and given me more knowledge of life, more experience. That is pretty good. I don't think there is now any particular disadvantage, really. People accept me as a person and accept *me*. Because I missed a lot of growing up, so to speak, I am still quite young, I can understand pop music and younger things. When I think of university, of course it is a disadvantage in that I would be a mature student, and some places don't accept them so readily. Possibly there will be trouble getting into a university. Sometimes I think that in the case of memory, there is a disadvantage in being an older student. I can't, perhaps, recall things as readily as some of the younger ones can. But on the other hand youth takes its turn anyway, so I just have to accept it. I think my performance is reduced in some ways because of my earlier drinking.'

Now that she lived with another woman, she said, she did not find herself looking emotionally or sexually at people with whom she worked. She knew that she owed a debt to the people who helped her. She said that she would like, ultimately, to enter the field of rehabilitation, so that she could help other people.

Possibly she had found her thoughts moved in this direction by her presence at the college. It had completed the process which began in the convent: her move towards recognising herself as a valid entity with qualities and obligations.

> 'It is tremendous, really. They take time out to talk to you. You feel you matter, and that is a great thing. They know you are disadvantaged, and how. In many ways, it is *alarming* as well as comforting. You think you have a particular sort of problem. You think, "Oh God, now I am facing this crisis." And in fact, they say, "Oh yes? Mrs So-and-so, your tutor, has been here for years and years and she has seen your problems over years and years." The difficulties become sort of minimised. I no longer feel delinquent.'

A few months after this conversation Yvonne became a student at a university, reading sociology and politics, as she had hoped. She said she was 'doing fine'.

The swan among geese

It is the feeling of being *different in any way*, objectively bad or *good*, which causes a sense of inferiority in the formative years. The swan is just as likely to feel inferior among geese as the goose is among swans. This may seem a psychological paradox,but it was clearly a factor among several people I talked to who had had to 'sort themselves out' as working personalities rather late in life.

A feeling of inferiority is not necessarily based on the sensation of being at a social disadvantage, as in the case of Yvonne who felt herself to be a working-class girl at a disadvantage to a new middle-class stepmother. It is equally likely to be based on an unconscious realisation of having sensitivities, interests and manners consistent with a *higher* social class. It is the simple fact of being *misplaced* that is dramatised into a feeling of being one-down.

Louise was the clearest example of this. She had a responsible job in industry, but was planning an undisclosed, more artistic, career.

I found an attractive woman of thirty, looking much younger. She had a rather dreamy face, gentle and diffidently intelligent eyes and a pleasantly cultured voice. She had the merest trace of a regional accent, and she was living with her parents in their small semi-detached house, not in the middle-class home and area that her appearance might have suggested. The home was full of inexpensive furniture, the walls bearing sentimental and highly-coloured reproduction pictures. It was the home of honest people without great claim to sophistication or knowledge of the world. The mother took her daughter aside at one point in our interview and warned her that I might be trying to sell encyclopaedias.

I asked Louise if, when she got her own home, her lifestyle would be the same as her parents. 'Oh, God, no!' she said. Then she added immediately, 'I'm not being snobby. It's just that I like things organised.'

It was a revelation of her own dilemma, the dilemma that had put brakes on her as a career woman and as a person: a battle between her personality and her loyalty.

Louise left school at eighteen. She had been through the sixth form, but 'didn't use it very constructively'. Was that because she had not been very interested?

> 'I *was* interested: I used to try very hard. I always used to get good marks. I was always in the alpha class, the top class, all the way up, but I didn't have much self-confidence. To put it frankly, I had very little self-confidence. I used to try very hard, but I didn't revise very hard for exams, because I never could believe I could pass them.'

Louise wanted to go on to art school, and had an A level in art.

> 'But I was stopped. My father wouldn't let me go. I think it was partly old-fashioned ideas, partly lack of faith in me, and partly genuine concern. My father took the view that all art students take drugs, are promiscuous and don't wash. The point was that he had never *said it before*, you see; so I had expected to go to art school. I was a very romantic eighteen year-old and I couldn't see myself doing anything else. I was very, very upset, actually, when I left school, and I was very much under my parents' influence then. When I was told I couldn't go to art school, I thought, "What *can* I do?" I couldn't see myself in an office. So I drifted from one job to another, six months to a year in each. My father and I had got on reasonably well, but the crunch came when I was 26. I started getting on very badly then, very badly indeed. You couldn't really say I had a first serious job – there wasn't one. My mum took me along to the Department of Employment. I think if they don't know what to do with a girl there, they push her into the Civil Service, so that's what I did. That was purgatory. Absolutely terrible.'

I asked her why it was so terrible and got an (from her) unsurprising reply.

> 'Because they gave us such inane jobs to do! They didn't give me enough work. There was the kind of atmosphere where, if the boss came into the office, you had to pretend you were busy. I just can't stand that, I really can't. I was not there long – I think I stuck it for a few months. It was hopeless, unfulfilling in every single way.'

She left home to live on her own in a much smarter suburb; but with no commercial training, took a job in a chain store. Then she worked at some stables, and then at a petrol station. Then she went into a record shop. That paid 'terrible' money, but she stayed for two years. This was some indication that she could fit better into any environment which was more cultural than her background and immediate prospects suggested. But at the age of 25, her earnings weren't sufficient, so she went into an electronics firm as a 'progress chaser', worked there for a year, and then undertook a full-time course in arts study at an educational establishment for women.

We were discussing her promotion to progress chaser – the first time she had been promoted in any job she had held – when I asked her whether (she would have been nearly 25 at the time) she regarded herself as a late developer. She said as far as self-confidence went, yes; and that brought us back to her earlier feelings of being out of place in her family.

> 'The capacity to do a job and the self-confidence to do it are linked,' she said. 'If you haven't got the self-confidence to believe that you can do a job, you can't really do it. I don't mean to put down my family, in fact, I am *not* putting down my family. But in our family, I am the odd one out. That is not particularly easy, for the parents or the child. For instance, my younger brother resents it a great deal. I never realised that until I was seventeen. We went to the same secondary school and it stuck out like a sore thumb. I have had a lot of resentment and aggro from my younger brother, which isn't very pleasant. Quite frankly, I wasn't being encouraged. I don't think they realised, either, because I was very quiet. I don't think they would have done it on purpose. I started learning classical guitar, for instance, when I was sixteen. I got along very well, even getting up on stage and playing at school when

> I had only been learning for about six weeks, which was a bit hairy. My parents didn't encourage me. My parents were frightened I was an *introvert*. And I wasn't.'

Why her parents were so frightened that she might become an introvert, when that personality type covers approximately half the human race, was not easy for her to explain. She was now quite clear, however, as to the real situation.

> 'It was just that I thought I had nothing in common with anything else that was going on in the house. They misinterpreted it. They used to try to get me out of my room, but I didn't *want* to get out of my room. I wanted to be there with my classical guitar, reading my poetry and my books, doing my own writing and my own thinking. I never meant to be antisocial, but it was interpreted like that. You are not going to believe this, but since I was about three I have felt the odd man out. I suppose it is damaging to confidence, but on the other hand it can build a kind of strength, funnily enough. When I was living on my own, lots of people that I knew from school would ask, "Aren't you lonely?" And I used to say, 'No, what do you mean, lonely?' because I used to like being on my own. I enjoy my own company.'

Two things happened to strengthen Louise's confidence in the year she decided to go on a full-time course: she got her first promotion, and she fell in love seriously for the first time. It was falling in love that rid her of a delusion about herself that had previously dogged her confidence.

This visibly attractive girl thought herself plain. The illusion of being ill-favoured in appearance is of course a common one among the unloved or misunderstood; but Louise did not know that at the time.

'I had always grown up to believe I was plain. I suppose I am, but my boy friend didn't think so. The point is, it gave me self-confidence. I was beginning to find myself in other ways. I can't explain it. You see, all my life people have been coming to me for advice, ever since I was at school. And it suddenly began to get through to me. I thought, "There must be something to me. People must think something of me. I must be worth more than I had previously believed." I saw an advertisement for a women's college and it said, "No qualifications needed." So I thought, well, what had I got to lose?'

Louise left the college before the completion of her course, having decided to work towards a freelance occupation which she would not discuss at the time of our interview, "in case it fails". But she said she believed that the growing confidence that took her to the college was also helping her in her new project. The fact of having gone to college had enabled her to get a job as chief information clerk to a professional man, and had probably impressed her present industrial employers enough to offer her a more responsible job than the one she had had before.

Louise's story was not yet an entirely happy one; and some of the strain caused by the difference between her background and her temperament perhaps still remained. Perhaps it will always remain? When it was suggested to her that her parents were working class in background, whereas she had interests more often associated with the middleclass, she demurred.

'I don't know. I think that's a bit snobby, actually, to suggest that just because you love things like art and music, that these are middle-class interests. Well, I am not fashion-conscious, as you can see. I am not a materialistic person. It would have helped if one had had people around one from the start who could

> have shared one's interests. But, then, life isn't perfect. What you have to do is try to see through all these things and compensate. They *shouldn't* affect you eventually. It is no good sitting and moaning about all the time you have wasted. You have just got to get on with it.'

Louise still showed a great reluctance to *seem* to be criticising other people for being different from her – even when it might have made it easier for her own ego had she done so, and might have been justified, in fact.

She said, for instance, that she 'didn't mean it as a put-down' when she recalled that, as a child in infants' school, she always seemed to be watching from the outside; and that what the other children were doing seemed to her a bit childish. One day, she said, the children had made a circle round her and shouted out a play on her name, as children would; a teacher had passed and smiled and shrugged, and she had smiled and shrugged back as she waited for the children to finish. She had then realised that she was identifying more with the teacher than with the other children.

> 'Now that I have discovered myself more, I can get on better with my background,' she insisted. 'I can accept it more. I was never ashamed of it, it is just that I couldn't identify with it.'

I asked her which childhood experiences she had found most restricting. She said she could not pick out one big thing, but lots and lots of little things had undermined her confidence and made her feel misplaced.

> 'It was trying to discuss things with other people in the family, and realising they didn't know what they were talking about. Again, I am not being rude. I used to lock my door just to keep them out, because I couldn't stand the frustration. I would be reading a

book or writing a poem and my parents would be banging on the door, and saying, "Come downstairs, come and socialise, otherwise you will turn into an introvert. Come down this instant." I would have to come down and sit with them in the dark, watching television. That's supposed to be socialising? It was hopeless.'

The path to progress for the swan among geese is invariably the realisation that admitting the truth about loved human beings need not imply disloyalty. Louise, who was discussing the possibility of getting her own flat (which with her more responsible job in industry she could now afford), was conscious that her success in her undisclosed new project was more likely because this fact was slowly filtering through.

Louise's view of her background was essentially a kindly one, which suggested the presence of the emotional maturity necessary for a radical change of direction.

'By nature, I am a quiet sort of person, I think. Anything odd they don't like. They couldn't understand it, and I think it frightened them. I know they wanted me to be what they considered to be the norm, so that I would fit into society. They wanted me to be happy. But they couldn't understand that I am not like them, and I am not like their idea of what is normal. What I need to be happy is precisely the opposite.'

I asked her whether she thought herself ready to establish her own lifestyle and priorities.

'Oh, yes,' she said, with conviction. 'I have learned to sort out my priorities now, so it will be the hell of a lot easier. I have wanted to leave home since I was eighteen and I did three times, including college. But I still didn't know where I was going. It was still just muddling along. I suppose I am still muddling along now. But I am doing it in a straight line.'

Late starters

A significant proportion of people who have found themselves wrongly slotted describe themselves as 'late starters'. They take the view that they were ill-suited to their previous employment because they lacked sufficient encouragement and guidance at the right and critical time.

Such lack of encouragement and guidance may spring from a lack of love. However, very often it does not, springing merely from the fact that the potential of the child is greater than the intelligence or specific knowledge of the parents. In a sense it is a form of the swan among geese syndrome, but with the emphasis more on intellect than social graciousness.

William, the ex-journalist who became a barrister and lecturer, and whose economic difficulties in adapting to his new profession were described in Chapter Five, said he had been 'a late starter all along the line'. One of the strains had been the difficulty of studying for evening classes while living at home with his parents.

> 'There is a gulf between us,' he said. 'My parents lived in a council flat and I couldn't concentrate. I was the only son, and I had a sister who was much younger than myself. I really could not work at home, so I found a little room of my own elsewhere. Obviously I had to earn my living, and I couldn't be a reporter because of the evening work, so first I got a job as a salesman, and then I got a job at a small factory, being mate to an engineer. A pretty useless

mate, but anyway it simply kept me going. I used to work from 7.30 in the morning until about lunch time, the idea being that I could go home in the afternoon and study. It never really worked, because I was so tired by the time I got home in the afternoon that I hadn't got the mental resources to apply myself. This went on until I was almost at the end of my tether, finding it getting really hard. I had a little money, and I knew basically I wanted to go to university. And then a school teacher friend advised me about a college suitable for late starters. I applied and studied there for two years, doing a diploma in politics and economics. I was with others who had left school at fourteen.'

His parents had not been able to suggest any practical way out of his dilemma earlier, and their mental horizons were not broad enough to understand the need. He had attended secondary modern school and left at fifteen. He had a flair for writing and took what seemed an obvious first step – working for a Fleet Street news agency as a newsroom 'dogsbody', and then for a local paper. Then he went into the Forces to do his National Service, which was then still in existence in Britain.

'I should explain,' he said, without blaming anybody, directly or by implication, 'that my formal education began properly in the Forces. I took advantage of a number of subjects for O levels, as a result of which, I passed four or five subjects whilst in the Forces. That was my real grounding. I came home, wanting to study and go to university, but not quite knowing how to go about it, so I went to a polytechnic and did O levels and A levels. It was a terrible sweat: I was doing science subjects. Then a teacher one day said to me, "You know, basically you are an arts man, not a science man at all. You are doing the wrong

> subjects." For example, trying to do A level physics without any basic knowledge in mathematics was terribly hard. Although I have got my A level chemistry, it was really too much. It was like trying to build a house without a foundation.'

A perceptive parent might have spotted that William was on the wrong track. As it was, he relied for his moments of guidance on chance meetings with sympathetic and shrewd teachers. His sense of inadequacy when he came back from National Service was caused by knowing that he had not realised his potential. He was then 21, and it wasn't until he was 27, after much lonely effort, that he finally got to the college.

It is difficult to avoid the hard and unpalatable fact that if his parents had themselves been well-off professionals,his climb would have started earlier and been on the right lines more promptly. The rigidity of present-day professional regulations has an often penal effect on those who start out late on the right track, because of lack of good advice at the proper time. This is in spite of the fact that such people, because of their necessary force of character, may in the end be more effective workers than those who have found the going easier.

But William and others like him have been too shrewd to waste much time castigating their backgrounds or the ways of the world. In the tough uphill struggle that the late developer must face, self-pity is not an escape, it is an additional burden.

Behind at eleven

Though more easily spotted and understood, the feeling of being *below* the intellectual level of parents, or of brothers and sisters, can lead to late professional development.

Ralph, who was formerly on the family farm but then went into the probation service as a late entrant, left technical college when he was eighteen.

> 'I had a hotch-potch of schooling, *which I think was an advantage in the long term* although it did not get me on very quickly in the short term. I came from a bright family where all the children passed the eleven-plus except me. I went to a secondary modern, which was quite a good school, but not good academically. I needed to do sciences for work in agriculture, and all I did at secondary modern school was something called general science – and the master was interested only in photography.'

This initial reverse cast a long shadow. At sixteen, Ralph, who was by this time head boy, transferred to a grammar school. He found it 'rather rigid', which may have been the fault of the academic discipline or of his previous experience.

> 'My options for A levels in the sciences were either chemistry, physics and maths, or chemistry, physics and biology. The only two things I had done quite a lot of were biology and maths and I couldn't take both of those, so I didn't think I could do very well, and neither did the headmaster. So after a year of getting some more A levels I opted out for a technical college to do A levels, where I started doing botany and zoology and chemistry. I was doing chemistry O level and A level at the same time, starting from scratch. But after a year, I found I wasn't enjoying the botany and zoology very much. I thought I might not get the A levels for a degree, so I decided after a year to cut my losses and go to an agricultural

college. It was, fortunately, not very difficult when I resumed study at the age of 23 or 24 (for the probation service) because I was much more interested in what I was doing then than I had been when studying before.'

In Ralph's case, the Home Office were prepared to pay him a salary while he was on his training course for the probation service. It was this happy accident that helped him to get out of an unsuitable occupation at an earlier stage than many people, and was one instance of society actively helping late developers after recognising their potential.

Redundancy: the blow and after

Compared with physical, emotional and social suffering, misfortunes of circumstance such as redundancy may seem small. Nevertheless, they can be just as financially expensive and almost as psychologically destructive; and this is not a new phenomenon.

Everything had conditioned Quentin to expect a secure career. He was educated at a good school and Oxford.

At the outbreak of war in 1939, he joined the Army, leaving it in 1946 to do a Colonial Service course at Oxford. He went out to Africa in 1948, at the age of thirty, where he became an administrative officer 'up country', looking after districts.

> 'That means you are the general purpose administrator and central government representative for all types of administration: judicial work, repairing roads, building road houses, looking after the prison, running the police force, collecting central

government taxes, keeping good order and military discipline going and also running all the local government.'

This position was of the Godlike sort which would not prepare a man for the idea that he himself might be vulnerable.

Quentin's world collapsed with great speed through no fault of his own, but to political change. It was the sort of change, the increasing independence of what had been the British Empire, that was to deprive a whole professional strata of dedicated men of their security, while it enfranchised those who had previously little say in their own affairs.

Some found it difficult to adjust to new circumstances. Quentin, working for a charitable foundation when I spoke to him, said that he had developed attitudes when working for the Colonial Service that he had found difficult to modify.

> 'The chief attitude one acquired was one of enormous precision, because you were surrounded by unskilled people who had to be supervised and used. You might have a very unintelligent man with half a primary education running a treasury with revenues of quite a considerable size. You had to supervise him, using him simply as your hands and eyes; and one was personally responsible for every last halfpenny. So you accounted right down to the bitter end, whatever you did. You had to see it all through yourself. You had to use your common-sense, sense of humour and sense of proportion as well. It did give you complete self-reliance and also an intolerance of anything short of perfection. This was not because one's standards demanded perfection but because only perfection would *work*. Anything else was the beginning of a drift into chaos.'

This approach was not necessary, nor welcome, back in the United Kingdom.

The obvious question was about power. Did the degree of power the Colonial Service men wielded not corrupt them or at least distort them?

> 'People often think like that,' said Quentin, 'in the same way as they often think of the number of one's servants. In fact it was such an *obvious* pitfall that one could see it and could watch oneself perhaps falling into it, and take oneself under control. There was a bungalow provided, but no servants. We employed as few servants as we could get away with, because they were an expensive commodity. Our salaries out in Africa were not very high. I might have been on about £3,000 by the end, which in today's terms would be many times that. But, on the other hand, one had children to educate in the UK. Somehow, by hook or crook, they came out during the holidays or one's wife had to go out and look after them at home and this was very expensive. On the whole, I would say we were just about making out, but with very little to spare.'

Quentin's redundancy was more cushioned than the sort to be experienced through rather different political and social causes later: the resettlement terms offered to men in the Colonial Service were reasonably generous.

> 'One was encouraged to stay on for as long as one wished. Their government was quite happy to keep us on until we wanted to go. There was no subtle pressure deliberately used, but one could see one's work was no longer required. They had to do it themselves: the African could learn only by doing

the job. I am not now criticising what happened, but if there was a weakness in our handling of things, I would say it was in the way we fattened up and trained our successors. It was not a positive thing, it was rather done by default. In other words, Africans increasingly took over the jobs until we found ourselves, and I found myself, with a job in which no one was really very interested. It consisted of preparing policy for land tenure for the country, but they weren't prepared politically for anything on which a land policy could be promulgated. They didn't want any advice on land tenure, because the time wasn't right politically for it. I wasn't really doing a useful job for my pay, but just hanging around. They didn't want my services, really, so I came back.'

I suggested to Quentin that this process was as demoralising, in a quiet way, as more explicit forms of redundancy.

'It was the sense of not being needed: that is what finished me off. Some people stayed on for longer periods, but most left. One or two continued in various jobs like magistrates and so on, but I think very few were left four or five years later. I stayed on because I was curious to see how the country managed with independence. Some people would say it was going downhill but, in fact, they were developing their own approach to things. It was an exceptionally happy territory to work in.'

Cushioned as the change was for Quentin, nevertheless there was a snag, which was of more general relevance than most of the experience of a non-recurring group of men returning home from the days of Empire. This snag was his age – he was 46. This was the worst age at which to make a change from the Colonial Service, in view of the scales of compensation, which 'went up and up and then started going down and down and down, on the principle presumably that when you get towards the end of a reasonable career you were not entitled to much compensation anyhow.'

This arrangement in a sense mirrored life. In ordinary commerce and industry, the middle forties can be difficult years in which to make a move, because one will not be in the new job long enough to accumulate adequate pension benefits, and a cash refund, in the forties, of pension money paid by the man himself, as distinct from the employer, is not sufficient to make up the difference, especially in times of high inflation.

Quentin left with about four years' salary. He returned to the UK and had six months' leave while he answered offers of employment.

> 'I wasn't working very hard to find myself a job because I had my compensation money and I expected to take a year to find a job anyway. One I applied for was an assistant bursar at a public school. I was interviewed, short-listed and didn't get it. The other was with an organisation to do with the locations of offices. Again, I was short-listed but didn't get it. The third was being general secretary of a large group of architectural concerns. Didn't get it. The Army Officers' Association wrote to me and said that I hadn't taken any of the jobs they had suggested and perhaps I was expecting too much in the way of salary. I wrote back and said, "You haven't *offered* me any jobs." They hadn't: the ones I had applied for had been under the Colonial Service Resettlement Bureau. The Officers' Association may then have had rather red faces, because they wrote rather

speedily, saying would I care to put in for *this* job? I put in for it and got it."

This gentlemanly path through redundancy led to the charitable foundation, which spends the revenue from large investments, mostly on supporting fundamental research in British universities, but also on personal awards, bursaries, scholarships, fellowships and travel grants to senior academics. Quentin's job was principally to entertain, in this country, senior academics from countries receiving grants.

> 'I suppose I started by being more precise than is normal in the UK. I never quite got used to the very flexible system of budget control that seems to be the usual principle here where, provided you are more or less within your figures, that is all right. I have always worked to a much more precise evaluation, and so I was nit-picking in the early days, in a way that I realise wasn't expected or required of me.'

In spite of his difficulties in adjusting Quentin said he was glad that he had not continued in the Colonial Service. This was partly because of the difficulties of his family.

> 'When my family started looking upon Africa as their home, and spoke about "going away" to the UK, I realised it was time I got out. I knew there was no future for them – though in fact one of them went back. But without political independence there it would have been difficult for me to make the break. Whether the shake-up was good or bad would depend on the extent to which initially one had shaken off the dust of the UK. I had never done that.'

Quentin was near retirement age at the time of our interview. He said he would then prefer another job to 'settling down and growing a nice garden.' The job would probably be connected with his personal interests, such as old coins. He might consider working for a museum.

> 'I suppose it *would* be a good thing if more people could change their careers in the course of their lives. I don't necessarily say they would be more efficient as the result of it, but I think they would have a better life if they were periodically pulled up, completely turned inside-out and put down again. It would be a very good idea.'

Quentin, of course, acknowledged that many people would find it more difficult to solve their redundancy problems than he had.

> 'Nevertheless, I would advise my son, shall we say, to go for a job that would keep him busy, and with the feeling that he was doing something worthwhile. I don't think I could possibly be happy doing something which in my heart of hearts I thought was a waste of time. It is not only a lack of qualifications that leads you into boring jobs. You could be highly skilled and crimping someone's hair, or transplanting hair into bald heads, and thinking, "Good God, what am I dong here?" You would know that people can be perfectly happy without a scrap of hair on their heads. This sort of job is just not justifiable, it is footling. One asks how the most footling person, the jet-setter, who just lounges around the place, can keep his sanity? They have no real occupation at all except titivating their own appetites. I think people who, in their heart of hearts, don't justify their existence to *themselves* must be unhappy.'

The same almost puritanical, certainly salutary, tone was implicit in Quentin's idea of the mental attitudes necessary for a successful change of job.

> 'I think you need reasonably respectable principles, and you should stand by them. Then you need an interest – an opportunity to work with your mind and not simply do what you are told continually. Plus pleasant and interesting colleagues. I think I would ask myself, in looking at a possible new job, to what extent there was a human factor in it, and not just bricks and mortar . . . The main factor in getting on with other people is to get on with yourself. That would be a key factor in any job change.'

The needed push

Sometimes, even in the harsher labour market of today, redundancy may provide the necessary push to make a change that might have remained only an unrealised pipedream without it.

Gerald, the former worker in the theatre who got a job as chief security officer of a mine in Africa, found the job 'an extraordinary swan really.' It was the sort of job that could have claimed him for life.

> 'There was nothing to do, but live in a beautifully luxurious bungalow, mixing in the cocktail circuit of the embassies and that sort of thing. Fascinating, but nothing to do. So they asked me if I would take on – and which I eventually managed – a tour of the country by an acrobatic troupe of about sixty Chinese Communists. Absolutely fascinating! I had been involved before in putting on pantomimes at

Christmas and other shows. And the security job gave me money and personal security, or so I thought. I was about 46 at the time. The government took over 55 per cent of the shares of the mining company and the very first thing they did, overnight, was to withdraw the work permits of the three senior security officers. So the three of us left within a week.'

Gerald had three children, whose ages at that time were fifteen, twelve and ten.

> 'It was traumatic. Very much so, after fourteen years, and in view of my attitude towards the country. I had not exactly identified, but I had involved myself very much with the country and its people. I was very, very hurt that I was just thrown out. They had to have an excuse, so they said we were anti-black, and had done all sorts of dreadful things. That was fair enough. That was the excuse, and I can understand it intellectually now. At the time it hurt.'

But, said Gerald, he had realised afterwards that he had been in a rut. It had been a very seductive atmosphere. He had a home in Britain in a beautiful position overlooking the water, plus a beautifully appointed bungalow, two servants and a good salary in Africa.

Forty-six was exactly the wrong age to be out on one's ear. He had come home to Britain. For the next nine months the company told its employees to hang on until it got the situation 'sorted out' and its men reinstated. But after three demoralising months doing nothing, Gerald answered an advertisement for a warden of an ex-prisoners' hostel which specified 'qualifications not necessary'.

This move, which Gerald would not have considered but for his enforced redundancy, led to a demanding and poorly-paid job. But the job led, in turn, to his training to become a probation officer.

> 'It is an intellectual challenge all the time, a perpetual stimulus. I like it more than the mine, because you are making judgements and decisions all the time. I think perhaps the most satisfying thing I have ever done in my life is the theatre. Where I have been lucky is in going from one satisfactory job to another. That is lovely.'

The path between two satisfying jobs might easily have petered out in the African mine's 'incredible swan' but for the effect of the sudden redundancy.

Uncertainty can help

Uncertainty about the future can act as a trigger for action, even without the final fact of redundancy.

Sidney, the general manager of a housing association (a charity), might not have got there but for the uncertainty of his employment in local government. It was many years ago that the first rumours of local government re-organisation began to spread; Sidney began to wonder about his future. He was then deputy clerk of a council. The chairman was entertaining, as a guest, the chairman of a local council in Africa, who turned out to be looking for a new council clerk. A meeting was arranged between Sidney and the council chairman.

'There were so many uncertainties,' said Sidney. 'I thought I might as well go abroad, enlarge my experience and get a much better job over there. The salary in Africa was about double what I had been getting.'

After independence, Sidney stayed on.

'Delightful climate, very easy life and my wife loved the country. We went for five years and stayed for fifteen. I took over another council at the request of the government and trained the Africans to take over the jobs in the council. Having done that, I had trained myself out of a job – I was no longer required. I accepted that there were no prospects in local government because of Africanisation. I went to another African country for a year, on a short-term contract as clerk to a council. Once again, the Africans took over. There were no prospects there, so I came back to Britain.'

There were not many prospects in Britain either. Sidney was 56. He was obviously too old to re-enter local government, so he looked around for another career. He was not too fastidious about what he accepted at first, and this stood him in good stead later.

Sidney took a temporary job with a group of companies which bought up blocks of flats for renting. This gave him fresh insights that supplemented his existing knowledge of housing, gained from local government. He now (because of his redundancy in Africa and a none-too-suitable new job) knew quite a lot about both the public and private sectors of housing.

When the job of secretary to the housing charity was advertised, he applied and got the job. After two years, the general manager moved on and Sidney was appointed to take his place. He had turned the low point, after his redundancies and uncertainties, to good account.

> 'To some extent, there was a conscious act of adaptation, coming from local government to work for a private housing association, but not as much as one would imagine. Particularly at that time, the association, like most housing associations, was financed by local authorities, so the background of local authority experience was extremely useful. Nevertheless, it was a complete change: you were working for private enterprise. The security wasn't the same, but the motivation was much greater since it was a charity, and connected with housing the elderly. It was an extremely satisfying and very interesting job, providing houses especially designed for elderly people for rent throughout the UK.'

The change brought a new lease of life to Sidney. He got satisfaction from knowing how to cut through red tape and rigid procedures, finding that improvisation was the key; adapting to the changing government policies.

> 'There was much more room and much more need for initiative in the housing association. I found the work far more rewarding, because you have to take the initiative the whole of the time, and speed processes up. In this job you are processing each decision, without going to a political boss. I might ring my chairman and say, "Such and such a thing is happening, so I propose to speed the process by doing this and suggesting that the local authority do that." No problem at all. You are allowed to take the

initiative, and in fact expected to do so, to get local authorities moving. For example, there is one local authority, which I won't name, that is basically very aggressive, but had a legal department that needed constant chasing. By knowing the legal situation of local authorities, I was able to say to their legal officers, "Look, we will wait for your legal processes to take their time, but in the meantime we can proceed to build on that land. Because it belongs to you, you have got full security and so we will take that risk. We may not wait for the processing of the legal documents, and we can give the builder the go-ahead to start now." In fact, we built the scheme before we had the land transferred to us. It took twelve months to get the land, and in the meantime the scheme was completed. That sort of thing.'

Sidney said that, with hindsight, he might have gone into housing association work much earlier. However, he had been conditioned to local government, and would have probably stayed in it but for the uncertainty and redundancy he had encountered.

'In local authority work you start as a teenager and junior, and you get through the machinery, so you become used to it and accept it until you get *outside* it. Then you realise the follies of some of the procedures and the nonsensical delays, which you know you can circumvent. When you are *in* the machinery you just accept it as it is.'

Sidney's case is an illustration of how the chance of a second career, for people in general, would make for more personal satisfaction and social efficiency in later life.

‘I think that it would be better if people could change jobs without prejudicing their pensions. To some extent it has happened in local government, because the regulations have now been amended so that you can get into the local government super-annuation scheme at sixty, so you can go on until sixty-five and get five years. Nevertheless, you can change, you are not debarred because of the pension. But to change one’s job is a major problem, even with housing associations, because of the pension schemes. We are joined in a scheme that enables us to recruit from local government. Other associations have a private pension scheme and they find problems of recruitment because people cannot continue their rights in a private scheme. I think pensions are the main barrier to changing jobs late in life. People are taking a slightly more philosophical view of age as a whole these days: they look at you for your physical and mental ability rather than for your age. But then you find you come up against pension problems.’

Sympathy extension

One potential benefit of redundancy can be measured in human as well as professional terms. It is the extension of sympathy of personal identification with people in trouble. Lewis, whose path from the financial world to the probation service has already been described, was working for a City of London firm which got into difficulties. He was left ‘out on a limb, sitting in my flat thinking, “Bills coming in left, right and centre, and I have got no income.” I didn’t really know what to do.’

He got a job with an overseas bank in Britain.

‘Lots of people had been in the company for years,

> and I had potentially a very nice job. I think some were quite jealous of it. Anyway, that created a lot of arguments. I had a row with the vice president of the company, so I was shown the door once again. I was becoming disillusioned. To be fair, I think that if I could have been offered a job where, once again, I was allowed to take decisions and be in a position to make money – perhaps at the expense of others – I would probably have taken it. But it didn't happen.'

The fact that it didn't helped shape his character. Instead of taking another lucrative job in finance, he became involved with an organisation which ran an all-night hostel.

> 'I heard an appeal for volunteers on a radio station, and I can't understand why I rang up.' Then he paused and added: 'I think in a way I identified with their clientele. *I* had been homeless and rootless. I was pretty rootless at that moment and, as things went on, I might have been homeless . . . Anyway, I don't know what it was, but I went along and was accepted as a volunteer.'

Lewis might have become a rather glib financial manipulator, mixing only with others of similar type. It was his ill-fortune, used positively, that opened his life to newer and more generous possibilities, with a keener understanding of people in all their varieties and fortunes. He is not alone in turning ill-fortune to such positive account.

CHAPTER SEVEN: OVER TO YOU

Reading about other people in a plight similar to one's own can lift the morale. Reading about other people in a similar plight to one's own who have successfully done something about it may lift the morale even higher.

But whether the reader then uses that enhanced morale to *do* something about his own situation depends completely on the individual. It is certainly so in the case of changing jobs. Those interviewed for this book had taken very careful stock of their own personal circumstances before they acted, and had tailored their actions to these; but in the end they had taken responsibility for themselves and their situation and *acted*.

There is an 'indifference filter' at work here, which eliminates anyone who does not *feel* strongly enough to act. To determine *how* to act requires thought, but to act requires the impetus of *feeling*, and if that feeling is not strong enough, then perhaps the individual concerned is better off staying in his mis-matched niche in life until he is too old to care.

I do not mean to suggest by this that the people I saw who had made a success of change had done it because they were the sort of emotional people who easily fly off the handle or throw in the towel. Quite the contrary. People who do that too easily because of the emotion of the moment should think very carefully before contemplating a career change.

One of the things that struck me after meeting a wide cross-section of job-changers was that their story was not as dramatic, or even melodramatic, as I had anticipated it might be. This fact is in itself revealing. It seems that people who *actually* change their lives in any real sense, let alone their whole career, as distinct from merely dreaming about it, are rarely prone to operatic gestures. A calm, deliberate sense of purpose – based on strong feeling but not overwhelmed by it – is a far more common characteristic among them.

The question one has to ask above all is simply: ‘Do *I* have that characteristic?’

By the same author:

Non-fiction

The People of the Forces Trilogy:

Soldiering On

Ruling the Waves

Guarding the Skies

One Man's Estate

Parian Ware

Novels

Candidate of Promise

The Scandalisers

Winston Three Three Three

ALSO AVAILABLE FROM ROSTERS

TALKING TURKEY by Alison Rice (£5.95)

A lively and entertaining look at this newest holiday sensation. Travel writer and broadcaster Alison Rice has produced an up-to-date guide to the main Turkish resorts and Istanbul. Aimed at visitors new to Turkey it explains what to see, where to stay — and equally important, what to avoid. Includes basic Turkish phrases plus hints on making the best of the food, wine and shopping available.

VIVA ESPANA by Edmund Swinglehurst (£5.95)

Discover the real Spain before the bulldozers and industrialists have destroyed its natural beauty. In this comprehensive guide to Spain, Edmund Swinglehurst, travel expert and author, has provided a fascinating glimpse behind the veil of Spain to show you the heart of the countryside, its people, its culture and its way of life.

CHAMPAGNE ON A BUDGET by Patrick Delaforce (£5.95)

Champagne is probably the world's most famous wine — yet few people have discovered the sparkling region where it is produced. Wine expert and travel writer Patrick Delaforce shows you how to enjoy a trip to the Champagne region, suggests tours, visits to vineyards and gives advice on the wines worth sampling. Aimed at the independent traveller who does not wish to bust his budget this book includes lists of medium priced hotels and restaurants plus handy hints on enjoying your stay.

FRENCH RIVIERA ON A BUDGET by Patrick Delaforce (£5.95)

The land of celebrities, champagne cocktails and caviare is just waiting to be discovered. In this timely guide travel writer Patrick Delaforce shows that you don't need to break the Bank at Monte Carlo to enjoy a stay among the rich and famous along the world's famous Cote d'Azur. He lists medium priced hotels, restaurants plus plenty of advice on how to spend those sun filled days and fun filled nights.

BURGUNDY AND BEAUJOLAIS ON A BUDGET by Patrick Delaforce (£5.95)

Discover one of France's most beautiful wine regions without spending a fortune. Patrick Delaforce, wine expert and travel writer, reveals the true heart of the French countryside. Just one hour's drive from Paris lies Burgundy, famous the world over for its wines, but also one of the most beautiful and intriguing regions in France. For the gourmet there is the chance to visit the vineyards where Chablis and Beaujolais are made and sample local produce such as truffles, river fish, fine game and fresh fruits. Includes: regional tours, local wines and wine co-operatives, value for money accommodation and restaurants, places of interest, regional events.

GASCONY AND ARMAGNAC ON A BUDGET by Patrick Delaforce (£5.95)

Discover one of France's best kept secrets — the land of brandy, beaches and Basque cuisine. Wine expert and travel writer Patrick Delaforce reveals the heart of one of France's most inviting holiday locations. From the beautiful silver coast fringed with pine forests through to the inland villages, there is an alluring countryside just waiting to be discovered. Magnificent beaches, sophisticated nightlife and superb cuisine. Includes: regional tours, local wines and wine co-operatives, value for money hotels and restaurants, places of interest and regional events.

IS IT WORTH ANYTHING? by Stephen Ellis (£3.99)

Most of us have drawers filled with odds and ends. But are they worth anything? Stephen Ellis writes on the money pages of the Daily Mirror which gets thousands of letters from readers asking just that. So here for everyone who cannot bear to throw anything away 'just in case' is the book which will give most of the answers. Includes: toys, stamps, glass, jewellery, postcards, records and much more.

COOK AND HOUSEWIFE'S MANUAL by Mistress Margaret Dods (hardback £14.95)

With an introduction by Glynn Christian

Discover the world of Mistress Margaret Dods and the Cleikum Club. Mistress Dods was the founder of one of the first cookery clubs in the country and her manual, first published in 1829, includes the story of how the club was set up, over 1,000 recipes as well as hints on wine making, curing meats and making cheese. Glynn Christian says 'It is a real cookery book, a book for people who really like to eat. Comic and revelatory'. Recommended by Chat and the Glasgow Herald.

NEW FEMALE INSTRUCTOR (hardback £12.50)

First published in the 1830's the book was designed to be a practical manual aimed at turning every one of its fair readers into an intelligent and pleasing companion. It includes: dress, fashion, morals, love, courtship, duties of the married state, conduct to servants plus more than 100 pages of recipes. Lively, entertaining — the perfect gift.

THE SHARE BOOK (3rd ed) by Rosemary Burr (£5.99)

With an introduction by the Rt. Hon. Mrs. Margaret Thatcher

An up-to-date, completely revised edition of this bestselling guide to the stockmarket which has been bought by more than 50,000 people. Includes advice on every aspect of buying, selling and choosing shares. A full glossary, details of members of the Stock Exchange, Unit Trust Association and Association of Investment Trust Companies. Plus new rules on investor protection and unit trust pricing. The classic companion for anyone interested in stocks and shares.

YOUR BUSINESS IN 1992 by James Dewhurst (£6.95)

Chartered accountant, author and authority on business management, James Dewhurst has distilled his experience into this valuable addition to any businessman's library. What will the much heralded internal market in Europe mean in pratice to you and your business? The answers are inside. Includes: setting common standards, enforcing technical requirements, competing for orders from public bodies, distribution services, prospects for take-overs and mergers, new tax environment and much more.

HOMEOWNERS SURVIVAL GUIDE ed. Rosemary Burr (£3.95)

Recommended by the Financial Times, the Sun and the Times. Everything the homeowner needs to make the most of his or her investment and run their home cost effectively. Includes: choosing your home, arranging the finance, count-down to purchase, insurance, decoration, home improvement moving on and cost cutting ideas.